Martin Library, York PA

W9-BLG-791

Whole Grain
VEGAN BAKING

Whole Grain
VEGAN BAKING

More Than
100 TASTY RECIPES
for Plant-Based Treats Made Even
Healthier—from Wholesome Cookies
and Cupcakes to Breads,
Biscuits, and More

celine steen and tamasin noyes

FAIR WINDS
PRESS
BEVERLY, MASSACHUSETTS

4860342

© 2013 Fair Winds Press
Text © 2013 Celine Steen and Tamasin Noyes
Photography © 2013 Fair Winds Press

First published in the USA in 2013 by
Fair Winds Press, a member of
Quayside Publishing Group
100 Cummings Center
Suite 406-L
Beverly, MA 01915-6101
www.fairwindspress.com

All rights reserved. No part of this book may be reproduced or utilized, in any form or
by any means, electronic or mechanical, without prior permission in writing from the
publisher.

17 16 15 14 13   3 4 5
ISBN: 978-1-59233-545-9
Digital edition published in 2013
eISBN: 978-1-61058-751-8

Library of Congress Cataloging-in-Publication Data

Steen, Celine.
  Whole grain vegan baking : more than 100 tasty recipes for plant-based treats made
even healthier : from wholesome cookies and cupcakes to breads, biscuits, and more /
Celine Steen and Tamasin Noyes.
     pages cm
  Includes index.
  ISBN 978-1-59233-545-9
  1. Vegan cooking. 2. Baking. 3. Cookbooks. lcgft I. Noyes, Tamasin. II. Title.
  TX837.S737 2013
  641.5'636--dc23

                                                        2012030812

Book layout by meganjonesdesign.com
Photography by Celine Steen

Printed and bound in China

To Jim and Chaz, for their loving support, and for never saying no to our kitchen creations.

Contents

First Steps into Whole Grain Bakingdom

Get up close and personal with whole grains and better-for-you ingredients.

If you like to indulge in homemade goodness on a daily basis, but fear that refined flours won't fit the healthier lifestyle you're aiming for, this book is for you! We've created wholesome, delectable baked treats that you can bite into with a clearer conscience. Read on before getting your bake on.

Stars of the Whole Grain Show

It's no secret that whole grains contain more fiber, which makes for longer-lasting satiety and better digestion, and that once milled into flours, they retain their bran and germ, which are their most nutrient-rich parts.

If you're used to eating refined flour-based goodies, it might take you just a little bit to adjust to whole grain treats As your palate adapts to the fuller taste of whole grains, you'll discover a subtle sweetness and a broad range of irresistible flavors and textures. Just let your taste buds do the talking. Chances are, you'll have the same reaction we did and wonder why you ever wasted time and money on flours that aren't naturally wholesome.

Some of the flours used in this book and listed below aren't the kind you can pick up at the local convenience store, but they are easy to find in well-stocked natural food stores, specialty shops, or online. We suggest buying in bulk when possible, and storing the flours in airtight containers in the refrigerator, or ideally, in the freezer. When ready to bake, let the flour come to room temperature for about 15 minutes before getting started, returning the container to the freezer as soon as possible. As always, we favor organic flours (and ingredients at large) whenever they are available and affordable.

All flours have different properties and bring their own characteristics to baked goods. Because of that, we cannot recommend using alternatives to the flours listed in our recipes. If you do, the results could be quite different and not as pleasing as they were meant to be. For a closer look, keep reading.

Amaranth flour: Amaranth is a high-protein flour with a slightly nutty, maltlike, and buttery taste. It is best used in small amounts. Because it has no gluten, it needs to be paired with other flours to create baked goods with a proper structure.

Barley flour: Barley flour has a very mild taste, allowing the ingredients it is paired with to shine. This is a low-gluten flour, which enhances a soft crumb texture when combined with other flours.

Brown fice flour: Brown rice flour is slightly nutty in taste. Some people find it gritty, but we've had good luck with Bob's Red Mill brand, which is finely ground. This flour is also gluten-free.

Buckwheat flour: Buckwheat flour is rich in protein, gluten-free, hearty, and nutty. We've used the dark-colored kind in our book, as opposed to the lighter version, where less of the dark hull coloring the flour remains.

Cornmeal, corn flour, and cornstarch: Cornmeal comes in various grinds. We prefer to use fine in quick breads, but keep the coarse on hand for other uses. Coarse cornmeal brings a more toothsome crunch along with the sweet undercurrent cornmeal is known for, while corn flour introduces a cakelike texture to baked goods. This flour has no gluten and should be used with other flours for better structure.

Cornstarch is a thickening agent and binder made from ground corn. As with all ingredients, we strongly recommend you purchase the non-genetically modified kind.

Graham flour: This is a coarse whole wheat flour that works wonders in baked goods. It can easily be replaced with whole wheat pastry flour (in anything that isn't yeast bread) or any sort of whole wheat flour (white whole wheat or regular), if unavailable where you live. Do not confuse it with gram flour, which is made from chickpeas!

Millet flour: Millet flour is a versatile, gluten-free flour that can be used in combination with other flours in any non-yeasted baking. It can also be combined with wheat flour to produce lower-gluten yeast breads.

Oats (includes oat flour, oat bran, quick-cooking oats, old-fashioned): Oats come in many varieties. They have a pleasing taste, and the textures of the various grinds bring different elements to baking. In quick breads, oat flour has a delectable, tender crumb, while old-fashioned rolled oats bring terrific texture to yeast breads. You can make your own oat flour by grinding old-fashioned or even quick-cooking oats in a food processor or blender.

Rolled flakes: We've used kamut, spelt, rye, and oats in this book. Rolled flakes are made from whole grains, which are steamed, roasted, rolled, and flaked. They take on the taste characteristics of the grain from which they are made. If you don't have access to kamut, spelt, or rye flakes, use the more readily available old-fashioned oats in their place.

Rye flour: Rye flour contains some gluten, but it can result in baked goods with too dense a texture if used in large quantity. Pumpernickel flour is darker in color and more coarsely ground than other rye flours, and it has an even more pronounced flavor. We use both dark rye flour and pumpernickel flour in this book. If you can only find one kind of these two flours, you can substitute either for the other, because the difference will be barely noticeable.

Teff flour: Teff flour is best known for being used in injera, an Ethiopian flatbread. It is a light, gluten-free flour with a unique sweet and malty flavor.

White or regular whole wheat flour: White whole wheat flour is milled from hard white spring wheat, while traditional whole wheat flour is milled from red wheat. These two flours can be used interchangeably, so when a recipe calls for white whole wheat flour, know that you can use regular whole wheat flour instead without missing a beat. Many people prefer the milder taste and lighter color white whole wheat flour imparts to baked goods, over those made with regular whole wheat flour. Like all flours, these come in various grinds. We prefer the finely ground, which is similar in appearance to all-purpose flour. Coarser grinds will still work, but will take longer to absorb liquids.

Whole spelt flour: A cousin to wheat, spelt flour is sweet and has a nutlike flavor. It is high in protein and gluten, but the gluten is more finicky than that of regular wheat. This flour absorbs water differently than other flours do, particularly among different brands. We've found Bob's Red Mill and Arrowhead Mills to be the most consistent. Note that Bob's Red Mill tends to need more liquid than Arrowhead Mills does. However, if you take your time and follow the cues, adding flour as needed, you will have success with all brands. Note that there are different types, or grades, of spelt flour, which differ by the amount of bran they contain. Whole spelt flour is the most wholesome— and what we call for in our recipes—white spelt flour, also known as light spelt flour, contains little to no bran and therefore has fewer nutrients.

Whole wheat pastry flour: Whole wheat pastry flour is nutty and sweet like all wheat flours, and has become our go-to flour for any baking that doesn't use yeast. It works well combined with all flours. It's especially perfect for things like cookies and muffins because it yields lighter results than regular whole wheat flour does.

Milling Your Own?

Because many people prefer the convenience of using store-bought flours versus home-milled flours, we've developed and tested our recipes with commercially milled flours. If you choose to mill your own flours, it is best to prepare only the amount needed for a recipe to avoid rancidity. Note that there may be variations in texture and results when using home-milled flours.

Tips for Successful Baking

Baking, unlike cooking, requires as much precision as possible to get the best results. There are so many factors that can affect baking, such as weather conditions and variations in brands and grinds of flour. With that in mind, we try to limit the variables as much as we can. As always, the most important thing is to read the recipe from top to bottom before getting started.

USE A SCALE

An important key in getting the best results when baking is to use a scale to weigh all dry ingredients, such as flours and sugars. The good news is you really don't have to break the bank to get a long-lasting and efficient scale these days. Weighing dry ingredients truly is a far more precise method than haphazardly measuring them in cups. We also like to weigh ingredients such as vegan yogurt, applesauce, and especially nut butters, to avoid having to deal with the messy cleanup.

When ready to bake, put a bowl on your scale and be sure to use the tare to bring the weight back to zero. Spoon the needed weight of the first flour (or other ingredient) into the bowl. Use the tare feature to return the scale to zero, and add the next dry ingredient. If the flours or cocoa powder look clumpy, you can sift them as you weigh them. Simply place a fine-mesh sieve on top of the bowl, use the tare feature to return the scale to zero, and start the weighing process. Remember to use a different bowl if the ingredient in question needs to be mixed separately. Repeat until all the ingredients meant to be added together in the recipe are in the bowl. To be sure not to miss an ingredient, gather all the ingredients on the counter in the order of use and work down the line. (It's called *mise en place*—how fancypants is that?)

Our M.O. with Weight and Measurements

We use one bowl for dry ingredients and another bowl for wet ingredients, and we keep a smaller bowl or two handy in case a few ingredients need to be weighed separately. For each ingredient, we've listed our preferred method of measurement first to help your baking get off to the best possible start.

KEEP YOUR OVEN IN CHECK

Besides the scale, it's important to be sure the oven is fully preheated. Oven thermometers are inexpensive, widely available, and can become your new best friend. Just as the scale ensures accuracy of ingredients, the thermometer is the only way to know the oven is working at its best.

USE OUR CUES AND YOUR INTUITION

We've made every effort to include cues to help guide you when working with flours that may be new to you. Working with dough is a matter of feel: You'll learn to look for texture and other small changes in the dough. We encourage you to use our cues for different stages in baking and to think of the time frames as guides. All ingredients are different, all ovens are different, and all bakers are different, but if you follow those cues, you'll be well on your way to getting wonderful results.

RISE WITH CARE

When making yeast breads, it's important to give the bread a chance to rise in a warm place. The ideal temperature is about 80°F (27°C). Depending on the weather, we have a couple of tricks for you:

- If it's cool in your house, the dough bowl may be placed on top of the refrigerator to rise. You can also turn on the oven at its lowest temperature, turn it off after 20 seconds, just when it starts to heat, and place the covered dough in there, which will help it rise more quickly.
- On the other hand, if it's rather hot both outdoors and indoors and you're worried your bread will be ready to bake before you are, part of the second rise can take place in the refrigerator. This method can be used to slow any yeasted dough to fit your schedule. Just be sure to bring the dough back to room temperature and let it finish rising according to our cue in each recipe.

STAND BY YOUR STAND MIXER

We love to use a stand mixer with a dough hook when kneading bread dough, not (entirely) out of laziness, but because it means having to use less extra flour than with hand kneading. This is especially welcome when working with whole grain bread dough, because they have a tendency to be heavier and denser than white flour–based breads. The less extra flour used, the lighter and airier the final product!

A few of our recipes call for a stand mixer exclusively, but not many. Some brands of stand mixers are a bit of an investment. If you're on a strict budget or are a part-time baker who doesn't want yet another kitchen appliance to clutter the counters, it's possible to find more affordable ones on the market. If you're lucky, perhaps a generous baker friend or relative would be willing to let you borrow theirs when the baking mood strikes.

STORING YOUR BAKED GOODS

Once they are completely cooled, most baked goods can be stored at room temperature in airtight containers or wrapped in (preferably recycled) foil or plastic wrap.

Because the shelf life of baked goods depends on the climate of your home, and especially if you've experienced mold issues with baked goods in the past, you can store them in the refrigerator. Simply bring them back to room temperature before serving, unless noted otherwise in the recipe. We strongly recommend that moist items in particular, such as leftover pies or fruit bars, be loosely covered and stored in the refrigerator for up to two days.

About Fats

We've elected not to use vegan butter in this book and to stick to quality oils instead. Don't get us wrong: We love to add an occasional pat of vegan butter on a piece of freshly baked bread, but it's still a highly processed item that's not always readily available, and it can sometimes create mitigated results in baking, as opposed to the more reliable oils we've used. Note that as new dietary information becomes available, it is common for ingredients to fall out of favor. We encourage you to make the right decisions for both your diet and your ethics.

Coconut oil: Our favorite brands of organic, extra-virgin, unrefined coconut oil are Spectrum and Nutiva. This oil can be cost-prohibitive, but we love its subtle flavor and the slight butteriness it brings to baked goods. Whenever possible, our recipes will contain a note letting you know it's okay to use another oil in its place. In our recipes, we call for different consistencies of coconut oil, which we get from heating or cooling it. For reference, we consider semisolid to be the same consistency as slightly softened vegan butter.

Neutral-flavored oils: Neutral-flavored oils are perfect when it comes to baking, because they won't overwhelm the other flavors. Take your pick from corn oil, grapeseed oil, light olive oil, peanut oil, safflower oil, and more.

Sweetening Things Up

The natural, unrefined, or less-refined alternative sweetening agents we have used herein are slightly more beneficial than overly processed and nutrient-void white or brown sugar, because they do, to varying degrees, retain some of their micronutrients. Here is a list of the ones you'll come across when flipping through the pages of this book.

Agave nectar: Agave nectar is a liquid sweetener that has become a bit controversial to many. Initially it was touted as one of the healthiest new sweeteners, but later studies have concluded that it may be nutritionally similar to high fructose corn syrup. That's why we've used it only sparingly and offered other liquid sweetener alternatives every time it appears. We use organic raw agave nectar that contains no sucrose or maltose, and the lowest amount of fructose. In general, pure maple syrup may be substituted for agave nectar. Recipes that make use of agave nectar can brown more quickly in the oven, so keep a close eye on the goods when using it.

Barley malt syrup: This thick syrup is made from sprouted barley and is half as sweet as regular sugar, is gentler on blood sugar levels, and works well as a subtler substitute for molasses. In yeast breads, molasses or pure maple syrup may be substituted for barley malt syrup.

Blackstrap molasses: Made from sugarcane juices, this intensely flavored, calcium- and iron-rich syrup is one of the signature sweetening agents in gingerbread and other spice-based baked goods. We like to use it in yeast breads as well in small quantities, because it makes for a beautifully browned crust. If you prefer milder, sweeter flavors, use regular molasses. Pure maple syrup or barley malt syrup can also be substituted for molasses, but keep in mind the results will be slightly sweeter as well.

Brown rice syrup: Just like barley malt syrup, brown rice syrup is half as sweet as regular sugar. We especially love to use it in applications where a caramel-like flavor is desired.

Coconut sugar: We find that this minimally processed sugar is intensely sweet before baking, but it tends to mellow once baked. For that reason, we often choose to combine it with another sweetener in our baked goods. It is sold under various brands. We prefer the sugar with only one ingredient: either coconut sap or coconut nectar. Sucanat may be substituted for coconut sugar and will yield a slightly sweeter result.

Organic evaporated cane juice: Free of chemicals and pesticides, this unrefined granulated sugar is slightly less processed than turbinado sugar. If you prefer, use it anywhere turbinado sugar Is called for in our recipes. Be sure to use the powdered kind for glazes. We favor the Wholesome Sweeteners brand because it is not only guaranteed to be vegan but is also fair trade.

Organic turbinado sugar: Instantly recognizable with its rather large crystals, this unrefined sugar is less intense in flavor than Sucanat but still retains molasses and an infinitesimal amount of vitamins and minerals. We use the Wholesome Sweeteners brand here, too.

Pure maple syrup: This syrup is tapped from maple trees. It is one of the tastiest, least refined, but also most expensive liquid sweeteners on the market. That's why we store ours in the refrigerator between uses to prevent mold. We prefer Grade B, which is slightly less expensive, yet has a bolder flavor than Grade A.

Sucanat: Sucanat is actually a brand name (standing for **Su**gar **Ca**ne **Nat**ural). This granular and flavorful sugar contains all of the sugarcane's molasses, which makes it a healthier alternative to regular brown sugar. If Sucanat is not available where you live, muscovado sugar is a perfect substitute for it.

Instant or Active? It's All Yeast to Me!

We've used active dry yeast in most of our recipes. If you prefer instant yeast, you know its advantage is that it doesn't need to be proofed before use, and can simply be added to the dry ingredients during preparation. We must confess to being active dry yeast daredevils sometimes: We don't always bother proofing it when it has worked in other recent recipes, and we've never had issues doing so. When in doubt, play it safe, follow our instructions, and proof your active dry yeast.

Both types of yeast can be stored for 6 months at room temperature and in the refrigerator, or for over a year in the freezer. While some yeast can work well coming straight out of the freezer, it's not always the case with every brand. Read the instructions on the package, and if nothing is mentioned, remove the amount of yeast you need from the freezer, letting it come back to room temperature before use.

If you prefer to use instant yeast rather than active dry yeast, decrease the amount by 25 percent. For example, 1¼ teaspoons active dry yeast should be replaced with 1 teaspoon instant yeast for the same rising time.

Vegan Milks: What's the Deal?

You'll see that we rarely call for a specific kind of vegan milk in our recipes. Unsweetened plain almond milk is our personal favorite anywhere vegan milk is called for, but all vegan milks will work well in our recipes, as long as they are unsweetened plain for savory applications, and plain or vanilla-flavored for sweet ones.

The only milk we specify is coconut milk, because it brings such a wonderful and unique taste to foods. For ease in baking, we've differentiated between refrigerated (the kind sold in cartons in the refrigerated section) and canned (the one sold on the shelf in, you guessed it, a can) coconut milk by using the words "refrigerated" or "canned." Simple enough!

Soy Freedom

If you are trying to limit your consumption of soy, all you have to do is make sure you use soy-free store-bought or homemade ingredients, such as vegan milk, yogurt, creamer, and chocolate chips. You'll see that a lot of our recipes can be made soy-free, except for the few that specifically call for tofu, or other soy-based ingredients, of course.

Chapter 2

Great-for-You Breakfast Goodies

Pancakes, granolas, and waffles: It's whole for you.

Making better food choices doesn't mean you have to start the day in a dull way. Enjoying whole grains first thing in the morning will help you greet the sun feeling more satisfied and ready to take the world by storm.

Lemony Spelt Scones

Spelt and brown rice flours join forces with sesame—in the form of tahini—to impart these delicate and zesty breakfast scones with an awesome nutlike flavor. Note that we call for whole spelt flour here, as opposed to light (or white) spelt flour, which has had most or all of the bran and germ removed. We occasionally like to skip the icing on these scones and make them all the more lemony by serving them alongside our lovely Lemon Curd (page 167) instead—plus a big cup of tea, of course.

• •

140 g (1 cup) whole spelt flour

80 g (½ cup) brown rice flour

1½ teaspoons baking powder

⅛ teaspoon fine sea salt

48 g (¼ cup) Sucanat

85 g (⅓ cup) tahini

2 tablespoons (30 ml) fresh lemon juice

2 teaspoons lemon zest

1 teaspoon ground ginger (optional)

¼ cup (60 ml) pure maple syrup

2 tablespoons (30 ml) vegan milk, more if needed

60 g (½ cup) organic powdered sugar

1 tablespoon (15 ml) fresh lemon juice, more if needed

Preheat the oven to 400°F (200°C, or gas mark 6). Line a baking sheet with parchment paper or a silicone baking mat.

In a food processor, combine the flours, baking powder, salt, and Sucanat. Add the tahini and pulse a few times to combine. Add the lemon juice, zest, ginger, and maple syrup, and pulse a few times. Add the milk through the hole in the lid, 1 tablespoon (15 ml) at a time, while pulsing until the dough is sufficiently moistened: It should hold together well when pinched and not be crumbly at all. Add extra milk if needed. Divide the dough into 6 equal portions, shape them into slightly flattened rounds of approximately 2 inches (5 cm) in diameter, and place them on the prepared baking sheet.

Bake for 14 minutes, or until golden brown around the edges at the bottom, and light golden on top. Leave the scones on the sheet for a couple of minutes before transferring them to a wire rack to cool.

Prepare the icing by combining the sugar with 1 teaspoon of lemon juice at a time, until it is thick enough to coat the back of a spoon but still easy to drizzle.

Place a sheet of waxed paper underneath the wire rack to make cleanup easier. Drizzle the icing over the cooled scones, and serve. The scones are best when enjoyed the day they are baked, but they'll still be great the next day if you store them in an airtight container at room temperature.

Yield: 6 scones

Double Cranberry Scones

While baking, the aroma of these scones will have people flocking to your kitchen. We've spiced our scones, packed them with two different kinds of cranberries, and added a subtle orange undertone. These are bursting with flavor.

• •

180 g (1½ cups) whole wheat pastry flour

90 g (1 cup) oat flour

2 teaspoons baking powder

1 teaspoon ground cinnamon

½ teaspoon fine sea salt

23 g (3 tablespoons) sweetened dried cranberries

50 g (½ cup) fresh or frozen cranberries

½ cup (120 ml) refrigerated coconut milk

1 teaspoon apple cider vinegar

96 g (½ cup) Sucanat

45 g (3 tablespoons) plain vegan yogurt

2 tablespoons (30 ml) neutral-flavored oil

1 tablespoon (6 g) orange zest

1 teaspoon pure vanilla extract

Preheat the oven to 375°F (190°C, or gas mark 5). Line a baking sheet with parchment paper or a silicone baking mat.

Whisk together the flours, baking powder, cinnamon, and salt. Stir in the dried and fresh cranberries.

Whisk together the milk, vinegar, Sucanat, yogurt, oil, zest, and vanilla in a small bowl. Pour the wet ingredients into the dry ingredients and stir to combine. Do not overmix. Spoon a scant ½ cup (105 g) of dough onto the baking sheet. Repeat with the remaining dough, placing the scones 3 inches (7.5 cm) apart. Bake for 15 to 18 minutes, until golden. Cool on a wire rack.

Yield: 6 scones

Recipe Note
For even more orange flavor, double the orange zest.

Chocolate Cherry Scones

Sour cherries and chocolate are one of our favorite flavor combinations. These are sure to put a smile on your face first thing in the morning, or any time of day. Coconut milk brings a rich taste to these scones, and thanks to the oat, spelt, and wheat flours, they are fiber-rich as well. Kirsch is a cherry-flavored brandy that adds the perfect fruity punch.

● ●

¾ cup (175 ml) refrigerated coconut milk

1 tablespoon (15 ml) freshly squeezed lemon juice

2 teaspoons Kirsch

1 teaspoon pure vanilla extract

90 g (1 cup) oat flour

90 g (¾ cup) whole wheat pastry flour

70 g (½ cup) whole spelt flour

36 g (3 tablespoons) Sucanat

12 g (1 tablespoon) baking powder

1 teaspoon baking soda

½ teaspoon fine sea salt

74 g (½ cup) dried sweetened tart cherries

58 g (⅓ cup) vegan chocolate chips

3 tablespoons (45 ml) neutral-flavored oil

Preheat the oven to 400°F (200°C, or gas mark 6). Line a baking sheet with parchment paper or a silicone baking mat.

Whisk together the milk, lemon juice, Kirsch, and vanilla in a small bowl.

Whisk together the flours, Sucanat, baking powder, baking soda, and salt in a medium-size bowl. Stir in the cherries and chips. Drizzle in the oil, stirring with a fork so that some clumps form. Add the wet ingredients to the dry ingredients and stir to combine, but do not overmix. The mixture will be a little sticky, but not wet. If it is too wet, add an extra 1 tablespoon (8 g) pastry flour.

Scoop the mixture onto the parchment and wet your hands. Pat the mixture into an 8-inch (20 cm) round. Score with a knife into 8 pieces. The scones will not be cut through after baking, but these scoring marks will be guides for cutting them. Bake for 18 to 22 minutes, or until the bottom is golden. Let cool on the baking sheet on a wire rack for 15 minutes, then move the scones to the rack itself. Do not move the scones too soon or they may break. Let cool.

Yield: 8 scones

Serving Suggestions & Variations

- Any dried fruit may be substituted for the cherries. An equal amount of white chocolate chips or chopped nuts may be substituted for the chocolate chips.
- If desired, drizzle the cooled scones with the icing from the Lemony Spelt Scones (page 18), substituting vegan milk for the lemon juice.

Raisin Bannocks

When researching for this book, we happened upon bannocks. These small, portable quick breads, traditionally cooked on a hot stone, are thought to come from Scotland and date all the way back to 1000 CE. They've since become popular throughout the world, being made unique by each of the different countries that embraced them. Our version is a cross between a scone and a biscuit. We kept the traditional oat and barley flours, but couldn't resist adding raisins. Oh, and we opted for an oven.

• •

Nonstick cooking spray

½ cup (120 ml) vegan milk

2 teaspoons apple cider vinegar

60 g (¼ cup) unsweetened applesauce

120 g (¾ cup) raisins, divided

3 tablespoons (45 ml) neutral-flavored oil

30 g (2 tablespoons) plain or vanilla-
   flavored vegan yogurt

2 tablespoons (30 ml) pure maple syrup

20 g (2 tablespoons) coconut sugar

7 g (1 tablespoon) flax meal

150 g (1¼ cups) whole wheat pastry flour,
   more if needed

90 g (1 cup) oat flour

105 g (¾ cup) whole spelt flour

30 g (¼ cup) barley flour

12 g (1 tablespoon) baking powder

½ teaspoon fine sea salt

½ teaspoon ground cinnamon

⅛ teaspoon ground cloves

Preheat the oven to 375°F (190°C, or gas mark 5). Coat four 4-inch (10 cm) springform pans with cooking spray.

Combine the milk, vinegar, applesauce, 40 g (¼ cup) of the raisins, oil, yogurt, maple syrup, sugar, and flax meal in a small blender. Process until smooth.

In a medium-size bowl, whisk together the flours, baking powder, salt, cinnamon, and cloves. Pour the wet ingredients into the dry ingredients and stir together. Stir in the remaining 80 g (½ cup) raisins. The dough will be sticky. Dump it onto a floured surface and knead about 30 times, adding extra pastry flour as needed. Divide the mixture into 4 even portions. Press each into a pan, using wet hands to prevent the dough from sticking. Place the pans on a baking sheet and bake for 20 to 22 minutes, until golden. Let cool in the pans for 5 minutes, then transfer the bannocks to a wire cooling rack.

Yield: 4 bannocks

Recipe Notes

• If you prefer, these scones can be baked freeform. Coat a baking sheet with cooking spray. Divide the dough into 4 portions and pat into 4-inch (10 cm) rounds.

• These can be sliced and toasted, if desired.

Coconut Spice Granola

This spicy granola will make your whole house smell like pumpkin pie, which is a far more delicious way to make one's home smell great than lighting scented candles. Not to mention, oats are a great source of soluble fiber, vitamins, and even protein, so there's really no wrong time to enjoy a bowlful. Just be sure to keep a portion of it to make our Granola Teacake (page 68)!

- 240 g (3 cups) old-fashioned rolled oats
- 120 g (1 cup) walnut halves
- 120 g (1½ cups) unsweetened flaked coconut
- 1 teaspoon cinnamon
- ½ teaspoon ground ginger
- ¼ teaspoon allspice
- ⅛ teaspoon ground nutmeg
- Pinch of ground cloves
- 44 g (2 tablespoons) molasses
- 168 g (½ cup) brown rice syrup or other liquid sweetener
- ¼ cup (60 ml) water
- Pinch of fine sea salt
- 2 tablespoons (30 ml) melted coconut oil
- 53 g (⅓ cup) chopped dates (optional)

Preheat the oven to 325°F (170°C, or gas mark 3). Line a 12 x 17-inch (30 x 43 cm) rimmed baking sheet with parchment paper. Combine the oats, walnuts, coconut, and spices in a large bowl. Combine the molasses, brown rice syrup, water, salt, and oil in a medium-size bowl. Pour the molasses mixture over the oat mixture, and stir to coat. Transfer to the prepared sheet. Make sure the preparation is spread evenly so that it bakes evenly.

Bake for 10 minutes, remove from the oven, and stir. Bake for another 10 minutes, until deep golden brown. Remove from the oven and let cool on the sheet, stirring occasionally. Stir the dates into the granola, if using. Let cool completely before storing.

This granola will keep for up to 2 weeks stored in an airtight container, at room temperature or in the refrigerator.

Yield: Approximately 8 cups (765 g)

Serving Suggestions & Variations

If you're not particularly fond of walnuts, you'll be happy to hear that pecan halves, or even slivered almonds, will make perfect substitutes here.

Chocolate Sesame Granola

For serious tahini lovers only. (Although we have no problem if you decide to use another nut or seed butter in place of tahini.) We are huge fans of good ol' rolled oats, but we've also been completely won over by the other kinds of fiber-rich and heart-healthy flakes used here; they bring a welcome textural change to the breakfast routine.

● ●

48 g (½ cup) rolled rye flakes

40 g (½ cup) old-fashioned rolled oats

96 g (1 cup) rolled spelt flakes

40 g (¼ cup) brown rice flour

26 g (¼ cup) flax meal

⅛ teaspoon fine sea salt

85 g (⅓ cup) tahini

2 tablespoons (30 ml) melted coconut oil or neutral-flavored oil

¼ cup (60 ml) pure maple syrup

24 g (2 tablespoons) Sucanat

58 g (⅓ cup) vegan semisweet chocolate chips

Preheat the oven to 325°F (170°C, or gas mark 3). Line a 12 x 17-inch (30 x 43 cm) rimmed baking sheet with parchment paper.

In a large bowl, combine all the flakes, flour, flax meal, and salt. In a medium-size bowl, combine the tahini, oil, syrup, and Sucanat. Pour the liquid ingredients onto the dry, and stir until combined.

Place the granola evenly on the prepared sheet. Bake in 7-minute increments, for a total of 15 to 20 minutes, until golden brown all over. Be sure to stir every 7 minutes.

Stir the chocolate into the granola while it is still warm, to melt the chocolate and make sure most of the granola gets coated.

Let cool on the sheet before storing. This granola will keep for up to 2 weeks stored in an airtight container, at room temperature or in the refrigerator.

Yield: 4 cups (475 g)

More-Than-Maple Granola

The smell of granola baking is such a homey aroma. The cinnamon and garam masala are enticing and add an exotic touch to the perennial favorite. Oats are one of the few grains that contain lysine, an important amino acid, while flaxseeds are high in omega-3s. But the biggest draw for us is the clusters. If you're like us, you've just found the perfect recipe.

• •

160 g (2 cups) old-fashioned rolled oats

21 g (3 tablespoons) slivered almonds

13 g (2 tablespoons) flax meal

9 g (1 tablespoon) roasted unsalted sunflower seeds

1 teaspoon ground cinnamon

½ teaspoon garam masala

¼ teaspoon fine sea salt

80 g (⅓ cup) unsweetened applesauce

3 tablespoons (45 ml) pure maple syrup

2 tablespoons (30 ml) neutral-flavored oil

24 g (2 tablespoons) Sucanat

1 teaspoon pure vanilla extract

60 g (½ cup) dried sweetened tart cherries, chopped

Preheat the oven to 300°F (150°C, or gas mark 2). Line a 12 x 17-inch (30 x 43 cm) rimmed baking sheet with parchment paper.

Combine the oats, almonds, flax meal, sunflower seeds, cinnamon, garam masala, and salt in a large bowl.

Combine the applesauce, maple syrup, oil, Sucanat, and vanilla in a small bowl. Whisk together. Pour into the oat mixture and stir to coat. Spread the mixture out on the baking sheet. Leave some space between the clumps, but try to get a fairly even depth so that the granola can bake evenly. Bake for 20 minutes. Remove from the oven, and using a spatula, turn the granola over similar to flipping pancakes. Bake for 15 to 20 minutes more, until golden. Remove from the oven and let cool on the sheet. The granola crisps as it cools. When cool, break the clusters apart as desired and stir in the cherries. The granola can be stored covered at room temperature for 2 weeks.

Yield: 4 cups (368 g)

Serving Suggestions & Variations

Feel free to substitute raisins for the cherries to make a more traditional granola. Or add your favorite dried fruit.

Morning Boost Muesli

We know, we know: There's technically nothing baked about muesli, but this is a whole grain book after all, and we love muesli too much not to sneak in a recipe for it. Loaded with cracked wheat, wheat germ, heart-healthy spelt flakes, and pleasantly chewy kamut flakes, this breakfast will ensure you won't get hungry again before lunch.

. . . .

1 cup (235 ml) water

53 g (⅓ cup) dry cracked wheat

Pinch of fine sea salt

240 g (1 cup) plain or vanilla-flavored vegan yogurt

1 cup (235 ml) unsweetened pineapple juice

24 g (¼ cup) rolled spelt flakes

24 g (¼ cup) rolled kamut flakes

20 g (2 heaping tablespoons) date crumbles or chopped dried cranberries

25 g (¼ cup) pecans, broken into smaller pieces

16 g (2 tablespoons) wheat germ

Combine the water, cracked wheat, and salt in a medium saucepan, and bring to a boil. Lower the heat, cover with a lid, and cook until the water is absorbed, about 10 minutes. Remove from the heat and set aside to cool slightly while preparing the rest.

Combine yogurt, juice, spelt and kamut flakes, dates, pecans, and wheat germ in a large bowl. Stir the cooked cracked wheat into the muesli, cover with plastic wrap, and refrigerate overnight to let the flakes plump up. Stir the muesli again before serving. Eventual leftovers will keep well for up to 2 days after preparation when stored in an airtight container in the refrigerator; stir before serving.

Yield: 3 cups (855 g), 2 large to 4 more modest servings

Serving Suggestions & Variations

- For a fruitier muesli, add 248 g (1½ cups) of fresh pineapple chunks, chopping them finely before stirring them in. Other fruits, such as fresh or thawed berries, would also be fantastic when added upon serving, to further increase the fiber and vitamin profile of this healthy breakfast.

Recipe Note

Date crumbles are nuggets made from dried dates, with only oat flour added to prevent clumping. They're ideal to use in baked goods because there's no sticky chopping involved, but you can replace them with regular chopped dates without missing a beat.

Baked Speculoos Doughnuts

Buttery, spicy, and caramel-y speculoos cookies were initially popular in the Netherlands and Belgium, but have become a worldwide sensation in recent years. It didn't take long for creative minds to turn them into the delicious spread we're using in these irresistibly tender, chocolate-glazed doughnuts. For a homemade vegan speculoos spread recipe, visit www.seitanismymotor.com. The store-bought brands Biscoff and its European counterpart, Lotus, are both vegan.

FOR DOUGHNUTS:

Nonstick cooking spray

1 cup (235 ml) vegan milk

144 g (¾ cup) Sucanat

2½ teaspoons ground cinnamon or speculoos spice mix

½ teaspoon fine sea salt

¼ cup (60 ml) neutral-flavored oil

170 g (¾ cup) plain or vanilla-flavored vegan yogurt

180 g (¾ cup) vegan speculoos spread

300 g (2½ cups) whole wheat pastry flour

12 g (1 tablespoon) baking powder

FOR CHOCOLATE GANACHE:

6 tablespoons (90 ml) vegan creamer, preferably Silk or MimicCreme brand

176 g (1 cup) vegan semisweet chocolate chips

About 10 vegan speculoos cookies, partially crushed, for topping

TO MAKE THE DOUGHNUTS: Preheat the oven to 350°F (180°C, or gas mark 4). Lightly coat 2 doughnut pans with cooking spray.

In a large bowl, whisk together the milk, Sucanat, cinnamon, salt, oil, yogurt, and speculoos spread until perfectly smooth.

In a medium-size bowl, combine the flour and baking powder. Add the dry ingredients to the wet, and stir until combined.

Divide the batter among the prepared pans, about ⅓ cup (82 g) batter per form, and bake for 20 minutes, or until golden brown and firm and a toothpick inserted into a doughnut comes out clean.

Transfer the doughnuts to a wire rack, and let cool completely.

TO MAKE THE GANACHE: Heat the creamer in a small saucepan until warm. Remove from the heat. Add the chips and stir until melted and combined. Let stand for a few minutes until thickened enough to generously apply on top of the doughnuts, using an offset spatula.

Sprinkle the crushed cookies on top.

Yield: 12 doughnuts

Recipe Note

There will be leftover ganache. You can turn it into truffles by refrigerating until set, scooping small rounds with a melon baller, and rolling them in sifted, unsweetened cocoa powder. You could also spread the ganache on freshly baked bread.

Chocolate Stout Spelt Doughnuts

This is a baked doughnut that incorporates beer. No frying here. The pastry flour and spelt combo are showcased in a way that can fool whole grain skeptics, thanks to the generous cocoa flavor and the hint of spice. And maple sweetened? Yes, please!

Nonstick cooking spray

270 g (2¼ cups) whole wheat pastry flour

105 g (¾ cup) whole spelt flour

80 g (1 cup) unsweetened cocoa powder

1½ teaspoons baking powder

¾ teaspoon ground cinnamon

¾ teaspoon fine sea salt

Generous ¼ teaspoon baking soda

Generous ⅛ teaspoon ground nutmeg

1½ cups (355 ml) chocolate stout beer, flat and at room temperature

⅔ cup (160 ml) pure maple syrup

3 tablespoons (45 ml) neutral-flavored oil

30 g (2 tablespoons) plain or vanilla-flavored vegan yogurt

2 teaspoons pure vanilla extract

30 g (¼ cup) organic powdered sugar

Preheat the oven to 375°F (190°C, or gas mark 5). Lightly coat a 12-hole doughnut pan with cooking spray. If you only have a 6-hole pan, refill the pan with doughnuts after baking the first batch. Spray the pan before refilling with the remaining batter.

Whisk together the flours, cocoa, baking powder, cinnamon, salt, baking soda, and nutmeg in a large bowl.

Whisk together the beer, maple syrup, oil, yogurt, and vanilla in a medium-size bowl. Pour the wet ingredients into the dry ingredients and stir together. Spoon ⅓ cup (85 g) batter into each of the doughnut forms. Smooth the batter and wipe any excess off the center part of the doughnut form. Bake for 17 to 19 minutes, until they spring back when touched. Let cool in the pan for 5 minutes, then transfer to a wire rack to finish cooling.

Dust with the powdered sugar just before serving.

Yield: 12 doughnuts

Serving Suggestions & Variations

For Chocolate Stout Spelt Peanut Doughnuts, frost the doughnuts with chocolate ganache (page 142) and dip them in 110 g (¾ cup) dry-roasted unsalted peanuts, chopped. What's better than peanuts and beer? Peanuts, beer, and chocolate in doughnut form.

Five-Grain Waffles

Packed with multigrain goodness, these hearty-tasting waffles will satisfy you until lunchtime, and even beyond. Buttery barley flour and sweet corn flour cozy up to the others for a perfect breakfast. Serve them with fresh sliced strawberries, or go traditional with maple syrup.

· ·

180 g (1½ cups) whole wheat pastry flour

70 g (½ cup) whole spelt flour

60 g (½ cup) corn flour (see page 10)

30 g (¼ cup) barley flour

24 g (¼ cup) oat bran

24 g (2 tablespoons) baking powder

1½ teaspoons ground cinnamon

Scant ½ teaspoon fine sea salt

1½ cups (355 ml) vegan milk

¼ cup (60 ml) neutral-flavored oil

¼ cup (60 ml) pure maple syrup

90 g (¼ cup plus 2 tablespoons) vanilla-flavored vegan yogurt

2 teaspoons pure vanilla extract

Nonstick cooking spray

Preheat a waffle iron to high. Preheat the oven to 300°F (150°C, or gas mark 2).

Combine the flours, oat bran, baking powder, cinnamon, and salt in a medium-size bowl. Whisk together.

Combine the milk, oil, maple syrup, yogurt, and vanilla in a medium-size bowl. Whisk together, then pour into the dry ingredients.

Lightly coat the waffle iron with cooking spray. Spoon a scant ⅔ cup (160 g) batter onto the waffle iron. Cook according to the manufacturer's directions. Transfer the waffle to a serving platter and keep warm in the oven while you make the remaining waffles.

Yield: 6 waffles

Recipe Note

These waffles tend to brown quickly, so be careful not to burn them.

Sweet Potato Waffles

Lightly textured with a gorgeous color, these waffles are a flavorful way to start any day. Three whole grains and sweet potatoes add up to serious satisfaction. Sweet potatoes and spice aren't just for fall—enjoy them year-round!

- -

10 ounces (280 g) 1-inch (2.5 cm) peeled sweet potato cubes

1¾ cups (325 ml) refrigerated coconut milk, more if needed

¼ cup (60 ml) neutral-flavored oil

¼ cup (60 ml) pure maple syrup

240 g (2 cups) whole wheat pastry flour

60 g (½ cup) barley flour

60 g (½ cup) corn flour (see page 10)

16 g (1 tablespoon plus 1 teaspoon) baking powder

1 teaspoon fine sea salt

1½ teaspoons ground cinnamon

½ teaspoon ground cloves

Nonstick cooking spray

Fill a medium-size saucepan halfway with water and bring to a boil over high heat. Add the sweet potato and decrease the heat to a simmer. Simmer for 10 minutes or until fork-tender. Drain and let cool until the cubes can be handled. Put the potato, milk, oil, and maple syrup in a blender. Process until smooth.

Combine the flours, baking powder, salt, cinnamon, and cloves in a medium-size bowl. Stir together. Pour the potato mixture into the dry ingredients and stir to combine. The mixture will be thick but should be spreadable. If not, stir in an additional tablespoon or two (15 to 30 ml) of milk.

Preheat a waffle iron to high heat. Lightly coat with cooking spray. Spoon ⅔ cup (180 g) batter onto the waffle iron and cook according to the manufacturer's instructions.

Yield: 6 standard waffles

Serving Suggestions & Variations

Looking for the ideal topper? Serve these with maple butter. To make maple butter, combine 1 tablespoon (15 ml) melted vegan butter with 1 teaspoon pure maple syrup and a pinch of ground cinnamon.

Sweet Corn and Blueberry Pancakes

These extra-easy wheat and corn flour pancakes are anything but basic. Corn flour brings a lovely sweetness, reducing the need for too much sweetener, which lets the blueberries and spices shine.

¾ cup plus 1 tablespoon (195 ml) refrigerated coconut milk

30 g (2 tablespoons) vanilla-flavored vegan yogurt

1 tablespoon (15 ml) neutral-flavored oil

12 g (1 tablespoon) Sucanat

1 teaspoon pure vanilla extract

120 g (1 cup) whole wheat pastry flour

16 g (2 tablespoons) corn flour (see page 10)

12 g (1 tablespoon) baking powder

½ teaspoon ground cinnamon

½ teaspoon fine sea salt

75 g (½ cup) fresh or frozen blueberries

Nonstick cooking spray

Whisk together the coconut milk, yogurt, oil, Sucanat, and vanilla in a medium-size bowl.

Whisk together the flours, baking powder, cinnamon, and salt in a medium-size bowl. Add the blueberries and pour the wet ingredients into the dry ingredients. Stir gently to combine.

Preheat the oven to 350°F (180°C, or gas mark 4). Heat a cast-iron skillet over medium heat. Lightly coat with cooking spray. Working in batches, scoop ½ cup (130 g) batter into the skillet. You will probably only be able to cook 2 pancakes at a time. If you have a griddle, you will be able to cook more at a time. Cook for 4 to 5 minutes, until the top bubbles and looks dry on the edges. The bottom should be golden. Turn the pancake over to cook the second side for 4 to 5 minutes, or until golden. Place the pancakes on an oven-safe platter and keep warm in the oven while cooking the remaining pancakes.

Yield: 4 pancakes

Fill-You-Up Oat Flapjacks

Flapjacks are a thinner cousin to fluffy, high-rising pancakes. This is a simple recipe, giving you the opportunity to add blueberries, diced apples, or another favorite fruit. Oats are a breakfast staple, but they don't always have to be in a bowl.

• •

¾ cup (180 ml) vegan milk

1 tablespoon (15 ml) apple cider vinegar

45 g (3 tablespoons) plain or vanilla-flavored vegan yogurt

1 teaspoon pure vanilla extract

24 g (2 tablespoons) Sucanat

45 g (½ cup) oat flour (see Notes)

30 g (¼ cup) white whole wheat flour

12 g (1 tablespoon) baking powder

½ teaspoon ground cinnamon

¼ teaspoon fine sea salt

Nonstick cooking spray

Vegan butter and pure maple syrup, for serving

In a medium-size bowl, combine the milk and vinegar: The mixture will curdle and become like buttermilk. Stir in the yogurt, vanilla, and Sucanat.

Whisk together the flours, baking powder, cinnamon, and salt in a second bowl. Pour the wet ingredients into the dry ingredients and whisk together. A few lumps may remain, and that is okay.

Preheat the oven to 350°F (180°C, or gas mark 4). Heat a cast-iron skillet over medium heat. Lightly coat with cooking spray. Working in batches, scoop ⅓ cup (75 g) batter into the skillet. You will probably only be able to cook 2 pancakes at a time. If you have a griddle, you will be able to cook more at a time. Cook for 4 to 5 minutes, until the top has bubbles and the edges look dry. The bottom should be golden. Turn the flapjacks over to cook the second side for 4 to 5 minutes, or until golden. Place the flapjacks on an oven-safe platter and keep warm in the oven while cooking the remaining flapjacks. Serve with vegan butter and maple syrup.

Yield: 5 flapjacks

Recipe Notes

• If you prefer cakier pancakes, add up to an extra 23 g (¼ cup) oat flour for a thicker batter.
• For really thick pancakes, add an extra 45 g (½ cup) oat flour.

Buckwheat Crêpes

One might think that using whole grains is a fairly recent dietary habit followed mainly for health reasons, but buckwheat is said to have been introduced in Brittany, the area of origin for crêpes, back in the twelfth century, where it was prized for its affordability and pleasant taste. We love to serve these hearty, yet tender and delicate crêpes with a little bowl of vegan yogurt on the side—or a scoop of vegan vanilla ice cream, when the mood strikes—and drizzled with the simplest homemade, unsweetened berry coulis.

FOR BERRY COULIS:

1 pound (454 g) any unsweetened frozen berries

1 tablespoon (15 ml) fresh lemon juice

Natural liquid sweetener of choice, to taste

FOR CRÊPES:

2 tablespoons (30 ml) melted coconut oil or neutral-flavored oil

16 g (2 tablespoons) cornstarch

1¼ cups (295 ml) vegan milk, at room temperature

1 teaspoon pure vanilla extract

Pinch of fine sea salt

2 tablespoons (30 ml) pure maple syrup, at room temperature

70 g (½ cup) whole spelt flour

30 g (¼ cup) buckwheat flour

8 g (1 tablespoon) chickpea flour

Nonstick cooking spray

TO MAKE THE COULIS: Combine the berries and lemon juice in a medium saucepan over medium-high heat. Decrease the heat to medium and cook for 10 to 15 minutes, until a thick coulis consistency is reached, gently mashing the thawing fruit while it cooks.

You can sweeten the deal by adding 1 tablespoon (15 ml) or more of your favorite liquid sweetener. Serve hot, warm, or cold.

TO MAKE THE CRÊPES: In a large bowl, whisk the oil with the cornstarch until dissolved. Add the milk, vanilla, salt, and syrup. Sift the flours on top, and whisk until completely smooth. Let the batter sit for at least 15 minutes.

Heat a 10-inch (25 cm) nonstick skillet over medium-high heat, move it away from the stove once it's really warm, and carefully coat it with cooking spray. Place it back on the stove and add a scant ⅓ cup (70 ml) batter, tilting the pan so the batter thins out and covers about 7 inches (18 cm) of the pan. Cook until the edges and surface are golden brown and the surface is dry, 3 to 5 minutes. Flip and cook for 1 to 3 minutes longer, until light golden brown. Transfer to a plate or wire rack. Repeat with the remaining batter to make 5 more crêpes.

Yield: 6 crêpes, and about 1½ cups (420 g) coulis

Serving Suggestions & Variations

For a super-thick coulis, add 24 g (2 tablespoons) instant tapioca halfway through the cooking, and stir occasionally, cooking until thickened. Instant tapioca is made of tiny pearls or granules, and should not be confused with tapioca flour/starch.

Apricot Cardamom Coffee Cake

This coffee cake is subtly sweetened, which allows the naturally sweet grains and spices to burst forth. Nutty whole wheat flour tastes richer when combined with barley flour, while oat flour gives this cake the perfect not-quite-crumbly texture. Spiked with dried apricots, the cake is topped with sweet and crunchy glazed almonds for a finishing touch and a delightful crunch.

• •

Nonstick cooking spray

1 cup (235 ml) vegan milk

1 tablespoon (15 ml) apple cider vinegar

¼ cup (60 ml) olive oil

¼ cup (60 ml) pure maple syrup, divided

42 g (2 tablespoons) brown rice syrup

38 g (¼ cup) slivered almonds

½ teaspoon plus a pinch of ground cinnamon, divided

120 g (1 cup) whole wheat pastry flour

68 g (¾ cup) oat flour

60 g (½ cup) barley flour

16 g (1 tablespoon plus 1 teaspoon) baking powder

½ teaspoon baking soda

1¼ teaspoons ground cardamom

½ teaspoon fine sea salt

97 g (¾ cup) chopped dried unsulfured apricots

Preheat the oven to 375°F (190°C, or gas mark 5). Lightly coat an 8-inch (20 cm) square baking dish with cooking spray.

Stir together the milk and apple cider vinegar in a small bowl; the mixture will curdle and resemble buttermilk. Whisk in the oil, 3 tablespoons (45 ml) of the maple syrup, and the rice syrup.

Stir together the almonds, remaining 1 tablespoon (15 ml) maple syrup, and a pinch of cinnamon in a small bowl.

Whisk together the flours, baking powder, baking soda, remaining ½ teaspoon cinnamon, cardamom, and salt in a medium-size bowl. Stir in the apricots. Pour the liquid mixture into the dry ingredients, stirring together. Mix well, but do not overmix. Spread in the baking dish. Sprinkle the almond mixture evenly over the top. Bake for 25 minutes, until golden brown. Let cool slightly before serving.

Yield: One 8-inch (20 cm) square cake

Raspberry Spelt Danishes

These pastries proudly feature a whole grain, laminated dough, which is prepared by layering dough (made from spelt, whole wheat, and barley flours) and fat (in the form of coconut oil) to create flaky layers of deliciousness. Filled with sweet raspberry preserves and topped with a luscious maple glaze, they are hard to resist. As hard as it is though, let them cool before indulging—you'll get the very best texture and flavor that way.

FOR DOUGH:

140 g (½ cup plus 2 tablespoons) solid coconut oil

140 g (1 cup) whole spelt flour

¼ cup (60 ml) lukewarm water

⅓ cup plus 1 teaspoon (85 ml) pure maple syrup, divided

2¼ teaspoons active dry yeast

240 g (2 cups) white whole wheat flour, divided

60 g (½ cup) barley flour

½ cup (120 ml) refrigerated coconut milk

45 g (3 tablespoons) plain or vanilla-flavored vegan yogurt

2 tablespoons (30 ml) neutral-flavored oil

1 tablespoon (6 g) orange zest

1 tablespoon (15 ml) maple extract

1 teaspoon fine sea salt

FOR FILLING:

320 g (1 cup) all-fruit raspberry jam

2 tablespoons (30 ml) pure maple syrup

1 teaspoon orange zest

FOR WASH:

2 teaspoons cornstarch

2 teaspoons pure maple syrup

2 teaspoons water

FOR GLAZE:

48 g (¼ cup) Sucanat

¼ teaspoon cornstarch

½ teaspoon pure maple syrup

1 to 2 teaspoons vegan milk

TO MAKE THE DOUGH: Crumble the coconut oil into tiny bits using your hands. The warmth of your hands will help slightly soften and break up the oil. Mix it well with the spelt flour in a medium-size bowl. The mixture should be very fine crumbs. Cover and refrigerate until needed.

Combine the water, 1 teaspoon maple syrup, and yeast in the mixing bowl of a stand mixer fitted with a dough hook. Stir together and let sit for 5 minutes to activate the yeast. Mix in 60 g (½ cup) white whole wheat flour and let sit for 30 minutes. Add the remaining ⅓ cup (80 g) maple syrup, remaining 180 g (1½ cups) white whole wheat flour, barley flour, milk, yogurt, oil, zest, extract, and salt. Mix for 1 minute, then add the spelt/coconut oil bits. Knead until a soft, smooth, and cohesive dough is formed. Add an extra 1 tablespoon (15 ml) water or (8 g) whole wheat flour if needed to make the right consistency.

Turn the dough out onto a lightly floured surface. Roll the dough into a 12 x 16-inch (30 x 40 cm) rectangle. With the 12-inch (30 cm) side against you, picture the dough in thirds of 4 inches (10 cm) each. Fold the left side over the center 4 inches (10 cm) of the dough, then fold the right third over that. Wrap the dough in plastic wrap and refrigerate for 1 hour. Repeat this process of rolling and folding the dough, turning the dough the opposite way at each stage, 3 more times, refrigerating the dough between each step for a total of 4 times. If the dough is too elastic when rolling it, let it rest for a few minutes, then continue. Wrap in plastic and refrigerate overnight.

TO MAKE THE FILLING: Stir together the jam, maple syrup, and zest in a small bowl. This can be made a day ahead and refrigerated, if desired.

Line 2 baking sheets with parchment paper or silicone baking mats. Divide the dough in half. On a lightly floured surface, roll one half of the dough out into a 10 x 15-inch (26 x 38 cm) rectangle, ¼-inch (6 mm) thick. Cut the dough in half across, then cut vertically 2 times 5 inches (13 cm) apart to form 6 (5-inch, or 13 cm) squares. Repeat with the other dough half.

With one point of the square pointing toward you, place 1 tablespoon (24 g) filling in the center of each Danish, spreading it in a vertical line but not reaching all the way to the points. Fold the right-hand point toward the left-hand point over the filling. Fold the left-hand point across the Danish and gently tuck it under the Danish to prevent it from popping open in the oven. Continue with the remaining dough until you have 12 Danishes. Cover with a clean kitchen towel and let rise in a warm place for 2 hours, until very puffed. For best results, use the oven rising method suggested in Tips for Successful Baking (page 12).

TO MAKE THE WASH: Whisk together the cornstarch, maple syrup, and water. Brush on the Danishes right before baking.

TO MAKE THE GLAZE: Combine the Sucanat and cornstarch in a blender. Process until quite powdered. Let sit for 10 minutes before removing the lid because it will be very dusty. Pour into a small bowl and whisk in the maple syrup, then add the milk, as needed, to make a glaze. Set aside.

Preheat the oven to 375°F (190°C, or gas mark 5). Bake for 13 to 15 minutes, until the bottoms are slightly darkened. Transfer to a wire rack and let cool, then drizzle with the glaze as desired.

Yield: 12 danishes

Recipe Note

Instead of refrigerating the dough overnight, the dough may be frozen for up to 3 months. Wrap it tightly in plastic wrap, then foil, and store in a plastic zipper-top bag.

Breakfast Pie Pastries

These naturally sweetened, pielike pastries are perfect for a filling breakfast on the go. They can be eaten still warm from the oven, at room temperature, or even chilled the next day.

• •

FOR FILLING:

200 g (10 tablespoons) all-fruit any berry jam

8 g (1 tablespoon) cornstarch

1 tablespoon (15 ml) water

FOR DOUGH:

¼ cup (60 ml) pure maple syrup

96 g (¼ cup plus 2 tablespoons) smooth natural peanut butter or any unsweetened nut butter

1 teaspoon pure vanilla extract

⅜ teaspoon fine sea salt

280 g (2 cups) whole spelt flour

½ cup (120 ml) vegan milk, as needed

TO MAKE THE FILLING: Place the jam in a small saucepan. Combine the cornstarch with the water in a small bowl and stir to dissolve. Add the cornstarch slurry to the jam. Bring to a boil, lower the heat to medium, and cook, stirring, for 4 minutes, to thoroughly thicken the jam. Remove from the heat and let cool completely before using.

TO MAKE THE DOUGH: Combine the syrup, peanut butter, vanilla, salt, and flour in a food processor. Pulse a few times to combine. Slowly add the milk, as needed, until a dough forms.

Preheat the oven to 375°F (190°C, or gas mark 5). Line a baking sheet with parchment paper or a silicone baking mat. We prefer rolling out the dough on a large silicone mat to avoid using extra flour.

Divide the dough into 8 equal portions. Roll out each portion into a 6 x 4-inch (15 x 10 cm) rectangle. Place 1 tablespoon (18 g) filling in the lower center of a rectangle. Fold the pastry in half to cover the filling, and seal the edges with a fork or your fingers. Place the pastries on the prepared sheet. Cut a tiny cross in the crust on top for ventilation. (For even prettier square pastries, roll into a 6½ x 3¼-inch (16.5 x 8.3 cm) rectangle, cut into two equal squares, spread filling in the center of one square, top with the second square, seal the edges, and trim with a pie crimper.)

Bake for 16 minutes, until golden brown. Place on a wire rack to cool.

Yield: 8 pastries

Serving Suggestions & Variations

• Lightly brush the baked pastries with a glaze made by combining 2 teaspoons cornstarch with 2 teaspoons water in a small saucepan. Add ¼ cup (60 ml) pure maple syrup and bring to a boil. Lower the heat to medium and cook until thickened, whisking constantly, about 1 minute. Or for golden brown results, just lightly brush the pastries before baking with pure maple syrup or raw agave nectar.

Lemon Ginger Rolls

We wanted a change from regular cinnamon-flavored rolls and decided to make these tender and zesty lemon ginger goodies instead, baking them as individual rolls rather than gathering them in a pan, which makes for even more of our favorite part: the outside crust! If you prefer the soft insides of rolls, gather them in an 8-inch (20 cm) square pan, let rise for 30 minutes, and bake for 20 to 25 minutes, or until golden brown.

• •

FOR DOUGH:

¼ **cup (60 ml) lukewarm water**

¼ **cup (60 ml) pure maple syrup, divided**

2¼ **teaspoons active dry yeast**

2 **teaspoons lemon zest**

¼ **cup (60 ml) vegan milk or water**

¼ **cup (60 ml) fresh lemon juice**

2 **tablespoons (30 ml) neutral-flavored oil**

210 g (1½ cups) whole spelt flour

180 g (1½ cups) white whole wheat flour

½ **teaspoon fine sea salt**

FOR FILLING:

36 g (3 tablespoons) organic evaporated cane juice

36 g (3 tablespoons) Sucanat

15 g (2 tablespoons) almond meal

1½ **teaspoons ground ginger, to taste**

TO MAKE THE DOUGH: Combine the water, 1 teaspoon of the syrup, and the yeast in a bowl. Let stand for 10 minutes to activate the yeast.

In a medium-size bowl, combine the remaining syrup, zest, milk or water, lemon juice, and oil.

In a large bowl, combine the flours and salt. Pour the wet ingredients into the dry and start kneading, adding extra flour if needed, until a smooth and pliable dough is obtained, about 6 to 8 minutes. Kneading by hand on a lightly floured surface or using a stand mixer fitted with a dough hook both work well here.

Cover with plastic wrap and let rise in a warm place until doubled in size, 1 to 1½ hours.

TO MAKE THE FILLING: Combine all the ingredients in a small bowl.

Line 9 cups of a standard muffin pan with paper liners. Fill the remaining 3 cups halfway with water to ensure even baking and to avoid warping the pan. Punch down the dough and roll it out on a silicone baking mat or on a lightly floured surface into a 12 x 9-inch (30 x 23 cm) rectangle. Lightly brush the whole surface of the dough with water. Evenly sprinkle the filling all over the dough, pressing down just slightly to help the filling adhere to the dough.

Cut the rectangle lengthwise into nine 1½-inch (4 cm) strips. Roll up each strip tightly and transfer it to the prepared muffin pan, with the coiled filling facing up. Press down to fit the cup. Cover and let stand for 20 minutes.

Preheat the oven to 375°F (190°C, or gas mark 5). Line the oven with foil in case the filling escapes. Bake the rolls for 16 minutes, or until light golden brown. Carefully remove from the pan and let cool on a wire rack.

We love to serve these rolls drizzled with the icing from the Lemony Spelt Scones (page 18), but you can skip this part if you want a more wholesome breakfast meal. The rolls are best enjoyed freshly baked.

Yield: 9 rolls

Banana Berry Breakfast Bake

Our breakfast bake is a sweet, peppy, all-natural treat that is served warm and eaten by the spoonful straight from the ramekin it is baked in. This particular recipe contains no added fat or refined sweetener, and it is a textural goldmine thanks to the addition of cashews, coconut, and pleasantly chewy, manganese-rich kamut flakes.

• •

Nonstick cooking spray

240 g (8½ ounces) frozen peeled bananas (about 2 medium)

90 g (¾ cup) date crumbles (see Note, page 29)

72 g (¾ cup) rolled kamut flakes

93 g (⅔ cup) raw cashews

13 g (2 tablespoons) flax meal

10 g (2 tablespoons) shredded coconut

2 tablespoons (30 ml) vegan milk, more if needed

1 teaspoon pure vanilla extract

¼ teaspoon fine sea salt

½ teaspoon baking powder

160 g (½ cup) Raspberry or Strawberry Curd (see Note) or Berry Coulis (page 38)

Preheat the oven to 350°F (180°C, or gas mark 4). Lightly coat four 8-ounce (227 g) oven-safe ramekins with cooking spray.

The frozen bananas will release some liquid as they thaw; place them either in a small saucepan over low heat or in the microwave. Stir the dates with the bananas; the warm banana liquid will help soften the dates. Set aside.

Combine the kamut flakes and cashews in a food processor. Process until no large pieces of cashews are left. Add the flax meal and shredded coconut, and blend to combine.

Add the banana-date mixture, milk, vanilla, salt, and baking powder, and process until mostly smooth, stopping once to scrape down the sides of the bowl. The mixture will be rather thick, but if it is very dry, add 1 or 2 tablespoons (15 to 30 ml) extra vegan milk.

Divide the batter among the prepared ramekins, approximately ⅔ cup (160 g) per ramekin. Use a chopstick to mix 40 g (2 tablespoons) curd into each ramekin.

Bake for 16 minutes, or until slightly puffed. Do not overbake. Let cool for a few minutes before diving in, because the curd will be especially hot.

Yield: 4 servings

Recipe Note

To make Raspberry Curd, see the Lemon Curd recipe (page 167), and simply add 125 g (½ cup) frozen, thawed raspberries (will yield tarter results than if using fresh) or 62 g (½ cup) fresh raspberries before blending the ingredients. To make Strawberry Curd, use 125 g (¾ cup) sliced fresh strawberries.

Chapter 3

Quick-as-Can-Bake Loaves and Muffins

Go with the grain while rising above it.

Whether you have a sweet tooth or a savory one,
these lickety-split wholesome wonders can be on the table,
in the lunchbox, or in your mouth in next to no time.

Puttanesca Scones with Barley and Spelt

Packed with salty olives and sweet, sun-dried tomatoes, these savory scones are tender and light. In winter, we serve them with minestrone soup; in summer, with gazpacho or salads. No matter the season, you're sure to find plenty of opportunities to put these on your menu. Or in your lunch bag.

• •

Nonstick cooking spray

180 g (1½ cups) whole wheat pastry flour

60 g (½ cup) barley flour

70 g (½ cup) whole spelt flour

28 g (¼ cup) minced sun-dried tomatoes (moist vacuum-packed, not oil-packed)

28 g (¼ cup) chopped kalamata olives

20 g (2 tablespoons) minced onion

12 g (1 tablespoon plus 1 teaspoon) minced capers

3 g (1 tablespoon) minced fresh basil or 1 teaspoon dried basil

2 teaspoons baking powder

½ teaspoon baking soda

½ teaspoon fine sea salt

¾ cup (180 ml) unsweetened plain vegan milk

60 g (¼ cup) unsweetened plain vegan yogurt

3 tablespoons (45 ml) olive oil

Preheat the oven to 375°F (190°C, or gas mark 5). Lightly coat a baking sheet with cooking spray.

Stir together the flours, sun-dried tomatoes, olives, onion, capers, basil, baking powder, baking soda, and salt in a medium-size bowl using a fork.

Stir together the milk, yogurt, and oil in a small bowl. Pour into the flour mixture and stir together. Scoop ⅓ cup (75 g) onto the baking sheet and lightly pat down. The scone should be about 1-inch (2.5 cm) thick and 3 inches (7.5 cm) across. Repeat with the remaining batter to form a total of 6 scones. Bake for 18 to 22 minutes, until lightly browned. Cool on a wire rack, and serve warm.

Yield: 6 scones

Savory Barley and Potato Scones

These delicacies have been compared to gnocchi in scone form. Be sure to use a baked potato that is not too mushy and soft, but just slightly underbaked instead. This is what will work in combination with the sweet and moist barley flour to give these their incomparable tender texture.

• •

120 g (1 cup) barley flour

¼ teaspoon grated nutmeg

½ teaspoon fine sea salt

160 g (½ cup plus 2 tablespoons) mashed potato (without skin, cooled)

1½ teaspoons baking powder

40 g (¼ cup) raisins (optional)

8 g (1 tablespoon) cornstarch

¾ cup (180 ml) moderately hot full-fat canned coconut milk

Preheat the oven to 425°F (220°C, or gas mark 7). Line a baking sheet with parchment paper or a silicone baking mat.

Combine the flour, nutmeg, and salt in a large bowl. Crumble the potato on top and work it in with the flour like you would cut vegan butter into a regular scone recipe, until combined and no large potato pieces are left.

Using a fork, stir the baking powder, raisins, and cornstarch into the flour until combined.

Still using a fork, add the coconut milk, a little at a time, until a dough forms; the dough should not be too dry or crumbly, but not too wet, either. Gather the dough with your hands and shape it into a ball. Divide into 4 equal portions. Shape each portion into a disk, flattened to 3 inches (8 cm) in diameter. Place on the prepared sheet.

Bake for 15 minutes, or until browned at the bottom. They will remain somewhat pale on top and look dry, but rest assured they won't be dry inside. Place on a wire rack to cool for a few minutes.

For a top that's more golden brown, toast the scones in a toaster oven before enjoying.

Yield: 4 scones

Serving Suggestions & Variations

We like to throw a bunch of raisins into the scones to get a little burst of sweetness, but you can replace them with 30 g (¼ cup) chopped walnuts or 25 g (¼ cup) chopped pecans.

Chipotle and Corn Spelt Muffins

These muffins are delicately spicy and wonderfully light and fluffy, just like you wouldn't expect from a baked good made from whole grain flours. That's just because whole grains really like to prove you wrong, in their own deliciously twisted way. Be sure to adjust the amount of chipotle pepper according to your preference.

• •

13 g (2 tablespoons) flax meal

16 g (2 tablespoons) cornstarch

1 tablespoon (15 ml) apple cider vinegar

1 cup (235 ml) unsweetened plain vegan milk

8 to 15 g (½ to 1 tablespoon) chopped canned chipotle pepper, to taste

2 tablespoons (30 ml) adobo sauce from can of chipotle peppers

60 g (¼ cup) unsweetened applesauce or unsweetened plain vegan yogurt

2 tablespoons (30 ml) neutral-flavored oil

135 g (1 cup) frozen corn kernels, thawed

60 g (½ cup) corn flour (see page 10)

140 g (1 cup) whole spelt flour

1 teaspoon fine sea salt

1 teaspoon ground cumin

1½ teaspoons baking powder

½ teaspoon baking soda

Preheat the oven to 375°F (190°C, or gas mark 5). Line 10 cups of a standard muffin pan with paper liners. Fill the remaining 2 cups halfway with water to ensure even baking and to avoid warping the pan.

Combine the flax meal, cornstarch, vinegar, milk, chipotle pepper, adobo sauce, applesauce or yogurt, and oil in a blender, or use a handheld blender. Blend until smooth. Stir the corn kernels into the mixture.

In a large bowl, combine the flours, salt, cumin, baking powder, and baking soda. Pour the wet ingredients into the dry, and stir until combined, being careful not to overmix.

Divide the batter among the prepared muffin cups, making each three-fourths full, and bake for 20 minutes, or until a toothpick inserted into the center of a muffin comes out clean.

Let cool on a wire rack. Store in an airtight container at room temperature for up to 2 days.

Yield: 10 muffins

Triple Onion Dill Muffins

These savory muffins take well to different herbs. Basil, rosemary, thyme, or parsley can all be substituted for the dill if one of them is a better complement to your meal. We love these alongside soups and salads, or packed in lunches.

• •

Nonstick cooking spray

3 tablespoons plus 1 teaspoon (50 ml) neutral-flavored oil, divided

79 g (¾ cup) minced leek

30 g (3 tablespoons) minced shallot

¼ teaspoon garlic salt

1 cup (235 ml) unsweetened plain vegan milk

24 g (2 tablespoons) Sucanat

1 tablespoon (15 ml) balsamic vinegar

150 g (1¼ cups) whole wheat pastry flour

45 g (½ cup) oat flour

30 g (¼ cup) barley flour

25 g (¼ cup) minced scallion

2 teaspoons baking powder

8 g (1 tablespoon) cornstarch

¾ teaspoon fine sea salt

2 teaspoons minced fresh dill

¼ teaspoon ground black pepper

Preheat the oven to 375°F (190°C, or gas mark 5). Lightly coat 9 cups of a muffin pan with cooking spray. Fill the remaining 3 cups halfway with water to ensure even baking and to avoid warping the pan.

Heat 1 teaspoon (5 ml) of the oil in a small skillet over medium heat. Add the leek, shallot, and garlic salt. Cook, stirring, until softened, about 3 minutes. Let cool.

Combine the milk, Sucanat, vinegar, and remaining 3 tablespoons (45 ml) oil in a small bowl. Stir together with a fork.

Combine the flours, scallion, baking powder, cornstarch, salt, dill, and black pepper in a medium-size bowl. Stir in the leek mixture. Pour the wet ingredients into the dry ingredients and stir to combine. Spoon evenly into the muffin pan, filling the cups nearly to the top. Bake for 18 to 20 minutes, until a toothpick inserted into the center comes out clean. Remove from the pan and let cool on a wire rack until serving.

Yield: 9 muffins

Savory Spinach Loaf

Packed with oven-roasted onions and swirled with spinach, this loaf is made with flax meal, which also boosts its nutrition. The barley and spelt flours add a little nuance to the whole wheat pastry flour. Pair it with a soup, salad, or our favorite—barbecued tofu, seitan, tempeh, or portobello mushrooms. Yes, really.

• •

Nonstick cooking spray

230 g (2 cups) ½-inch thick (1.3 cm) half-moon-sliced onion

3 tablespoons (45 ml) neutral-flavored oil, divided

1 teaspoon plus a pinch fine sea salt, divided

¼ teaspoon plus a pinch ground black pepper, divided

110 g (3 cups) packed baby spinach, cut into ½- to 1-inch (1.3 to 2.5 cm) slices

180 g (1½ cups) whole wheat pastry flour

70 g (½ cup) whole spelt flour

30 g (¼ cup) barley flour

13 g (2 tablespoons) flax meal

8 g (1 tablespoon) cornstarch

2 teaspoons baking powder

1 teaspoon dried oregano

½ teaspoon baking soda

1¼ cups (295 ml) unsweetened plain vegan milk

30 g (2 tablespoons) unsweetened plain vegan yogurt

1 tablespoon (15 ml) balsamic vinegar

2 cloves garlic, minced

Preheat the oven to 400°F (200°C, or gas mark 6). Lightly coat a 9 x 5-inch (23 x 13 cm) loaf pan with cooking spray.

Toss the onion, 2 tablespoons (30 ml) of the oil, and a pinch of the salt and a pinch of the pepper on a 9 x 13-inch (23 x 33 cm) baking sheet. Bake for 30 to 35 minutes, stirring once, until limp and starting to brown. Stir in the spinach and return to the oven for 2 minutes. Remove from the oven and set aside.

Whisk together the flours, flax, cornstarch, baking powder, oregano, baking soda, the remaining 1 teaspoon salt, and the remaining ¼ teaspoon pepper in a medium-size bowl.

Whisk together the milk, yogurt, vinegar, remaining 1 tablespoon (15 ml) oil, and garlic in a small bowl. Pour the wet ingredients into the dry ingredients and stir gently to combine. Do not overmix. Fold the spinach and onions into the batter. Pour into the prepared loaf pan and bake for 20 minutes. Cover loosely with foil to prevent overbrowning, then bake for another 20 minutes, until a toothpick inserted into the center comes out clean and the loaf has pulled away from the sides of the pan. Let cool in the pan for 5 minutes, then remove the loaf from the pan and let cool on a wire rack.

Yield: 1 loaf

Onion Caraway Whole Wheat Loaf

One of us (who shall remain nameless) went a bit shopping crazy and bought 2 pounds (908 g) of caraway seeds online. It will take a lot of onion caraway loaves to get rid of those seeds, but we're big fans of this recipe's speedy preparation, flavor combination, and tender yet firm crumb, so we'll happily make do. We're sure you will, too.

Nonstick cooking spray

360 g (3 cups) whole wheat pastry flour

12 g (1 tablespoon) baking powder

1¼ teaspoons fine sea salt

13 g (2 tablespoons) caraway seeds

10 g (1½ tablespoons) onion powder

16 g (2 tablespoons) cornstarch or arrowroot powder

1½ cups (353 ml) vegan beer, plus up to ¼ cup (60 ml) extra if needed

2 tablespoons (30 ml) neutral-flavored oil

30 g (¼ cup) salted, toasted pepitas (hulled pumpkin seeds), for topping

Preheat the oven to 350°F (180°C, or gas mark 4). Coat an 8 x 4-inch (20 x 10 cm) loaf pan with cooking spray.

In a large bowl, combine the flour, baking powder, salt, caraway seeds, onion powder, and cornstarch or arrowroot powder.

Add the 1½ cups (353 ml) beer and oil, and stir until just combined. If the batter is too dry, slowly add extra beer as needed.

Scrape the batter into the prepared pan. Sprinkle the pepitas on top. Bake for 50 to 60 minutes, until golden brown and a toothpick inserted into the center comes out clean.

Let cool on a wire rack before slicing. This bread tastes best when enjoyed freshly baked. We recommend you toast the eventual leftovers before enjoying the next day.

Yield: 1 loaf

Recipe Note

If you don't want to use beer, even though it imparts great flavor here, you can replace it with the same amount of seltzer water.

Toasted Garlic and Herb Bread

With specks of green herbs, this light pan bread is the perfect side to many soups, salads, and main dishes, but don't overlook it as a quick snack. After all, herbs and garlic are like a happy couple, especially when supported by a trio of whole grains. To get the most health benefit from garlic, mince the cloves at least 10 minutes before using.

Nonstick cooking spray

3 tablespoons (45 ml) neutral-flavored oil

4 cloves garlic, minced

1½ cups (355 ml) unsweetened plain vegan milk

2 teaspoons apple cider vinegar

240 g (2 cups) whole wheat pastry flour

70 g (½ cup) whole spelt flour

30 g (¼ cup) barley flour

24 g (2 tablespoons) Sucanat

8 g (1 tablespoon) cornstarch

2 teaspoons baking powder

½ teaspoon baking soda

1 teaspoon fine sea salt

½ teaspoon ground white pepper

6 g (2 tablespoons) minced fresh chives

8 g (2 tablespoons) minced fresh parsley

1 teaspoon minced fresh rosemary

Preheat the oven to 375°F (190°C, or gas mark 5). Lightly coat an 8-inch (20 cm) square pan with cooking spray.

Heat the oil and garlic in a small skillet over medium-low heat. Cook, stirring, for 5 minutes, until the garlic is toasted. Do not overbrown the garlic or it will be bitter. Whisk together the milk and vinegar in a small bowl. The mixture will curdle and become like buttermilk. Whisk the garlic mixture into the milk.

Combine the flours, Sucanat, cornstarch, baking powder, baking soda, salt, pepper, chives, parsley, and rosemary in a medium-size bowl. Whisk to combine. Pour the oil mixture into the dry ingredients and stir until just combined. Pour into the baking dish and smooth the top. Bake for 28 to 32 minutes, until a toothpick inserted into the center comes out clean and the bread has slightly pulled away from the sides of the pan. Cut and serve from the pan.

Yield: 12 servings

Spicy Cranberry Cornbread

A wee bit sweet, a wee bit spicy, and all very savory, this cornbread has the perfect crust thanks to the hot cast-iron skillet. Cornmeal is packed with nutrients, minerals, and amino acids. Plus, it tastes great! Start with this recipe, then tweak it to your taste. Double the scallions, jalapeños, or cranberries to make it your own.

• •

1½ cups (355 ml) unsweetened plain vegan milk, more if needed

1 tablespoon (15 ml) apple cider vinegar

60 g (¼ cup) unsweetened applesauce

2 tablespoons (30 ml) pure maple syrup

18 g (3 tablespoons) minced scallion

18 g (2 tablespoons) minced jalapeño pepper

15 g (2 tablespoons) dried sweetened cranberries, chopped

1 tablespoon (15 ml) neutral-flavored oil

120 g (1 cup) whole wheat pastry flour

60 g (½ cup) corn flour (see page 10)

88 g (½ cup plus 2 tablespoons) coarsely ground cornmeal

1 teaspoon fine sea salt

¼ teaspoon ground black pepper

12 g (1 tablespoon) baking powder

Nonstick cooking spray

Put an 8-inch (20 cm) cast-iron skillet in the oven and preheat the oven to 400°F (200°C, or gas mark 6).

Combine the milk and vinegar in a medium-size bowl: The mixture will curdle and become like buttermilk. Stir in the applesauce, syrup, scallion, jalapeño, cranberries, and oil.

Combine the flours, cornmeal, salt, pepper, and baking powder in a second medium-size bowl. Whisk to combine. Pour the wet ingredients into the dry and stir until combined, but do not overmix. If the mixture is too dry, add additional milk 1 tablespoon (15 ml) at a time as needed. The mixture should be pourable.

Carefully take the skillet out of the oven and coat it with cooking spray. Pour the cornbread batter into the skillet and put it back in the oven. Bake for 33 to 38 minutes, until a toothpick inserted into the center comes out clean. Let cool slightly before serving.

Yield: 6 servings

Savory Pumpernickel Waffles

Sure, we love bread as much as anyone. Maybe more. But these waffles are the perfect side dish when you feel like shaking things up, or just for a snack. We love the crunch that cornmeal brings and the deep flavor of the pumpernickel flour. The mustard adds a delightful tang, and sauerkraut makes these waffles pop with umami.

• •

60 g (½ cup) whole wheat pastry flour

30 g (¼ cup) pumpernickel flour

30 g (¼ cup) finely ground cornmeal

3 g (1 tablespoon) minced fresh chives

12 g (1 tablespoon) baking powder

7 g (1 tablespoon) flax meal

¼ teaspoon fine sea salt

Pinch of ground black pepper

½ cup plus 2 tablespoons (150 ml) unsweetened plain vegan milk, more if needed

71 g (½ cup) drained sauerkraut (not squeezed)

30 g (2 tablespoons) Dijon mustard

1 tablespoon (15 ml) neutral-flavored oil

Nonstick cooking spray

Heat a waffle iron to high heat.

Combine the flours, cornmeal, chives, baking powder, flax meal, salt, and pepper in a medium-size bowl.

Combine the milk, sauerkraut, mustard, and oil in a blender. Process until smooth. Pour the wet ingredients into the dry ingredients and stir together. Add 1 tablespoon (15 ml) milk, if needed, to make a thick but spreadable mixture.

Coat the waffle iron with cooking spray. Spoon about ⅔ cup (150 g) batter onto the waffle iron. Cook the waffles according the manufacturer's instructions. Waffles may be kept warm in a 300°F (150°C, or gas mark 2) oven before serving, if desired.

Yield: 2 waffles

Recipe Note

Try these waffles instead of bread in your favorite sandwiches! Reubens, anyone?

Carrot Cashew Loaf

This loaf is healthy enough for breakfast, yet sweet enough to enjoy with a cup of tea or as dessert. We love the rich base that the cashews bring to the recipe. With just the right spices, sweet carrots (your mom was right; they are good for your eyes!), and a hint of citrus, this loaf can be sliced quite thin thanks to its cakelike texture. Dust it with organic powdered sugar for a gorgeous (and easy!) finish, if desired.

• •

70 g (½ cup) cashews

½ cup (120 ml) orange juice

30 g (3 tablespoons) raisins

¼ cup (60 ml) vegan milk

3 tablespoons (45 ml) pure maple syrup

2 tablespoons (30 ml) neutral-flavored oil

30 g (2 tablespoons) vanilla-flavored
    vegan yogurt

2 teaspoons apple cider vinegar

¾ teaspoon ground cinnamon

¼ teaspoon ground allspice

Nonstick cooking spray

120 g (1 cup) whole wheat pastry flour

45 g (½ cup) oat flour

30 g (¼ cup) barley flour

110 g (1 cup) shredded carrot

12 g (1 tablespoon) baking powder

8 g (1 tablespoon) cornstarch

2 teaspoons orange zest

1 teaspoon baking soda

½ teaspoon fine sea salt

Combine the cashews, orange juice, and raisins in a blender. Let sit for 2 to 3 hours to soften the cashews. Process until completely smooth. Add the milk, maple syrup, oil, yogurt, vinegar, cinnamon, and allspice. Process until combined.

Preheat the oven to 375°F (190°C, or gas mark 5). Lightly coat an 8 x 4-Inch (20 x 10 cm) loaf pan with cooking spray.

In a medium-size bowl, whisk together the flours, carrot, baking powder, cornstarch, zest, baking soda, and salt. Pour the wet ingredients into the dry ingredients and stir together. Pour into the pan and bake for 30 to 35 minutes, until the loaf slightly pulls away from the sides of the pan and a toothpick inserted into the center comes out clean. Let cool in the pan for 5 minutes. Remove from the pan and let cool on a wire rack. Let the loaf cool before dusting with sugar, if using.

Yield: 1 loaf

Serving Suggestions & Variations

- If desired, 60 g (½ cup) chopped walnuts or 88 g (½ cup) vegan semisweet chocolate chips may be added to the batter.
- Top it with a drizzle. Try the icing from the Lemony Spelt Scones (page 18), substituting orange juice for the lemon juice. When adding a drizzle, put a piece of waxed paper under the wire rack for the easiest cleanup.

Autumny Apple Spelt Loaf

This is a moderately sweet, slightly dense (in a good way) autumnal kind of loaf that is perfect when served with a touch of apple butter or even quince jam, if you have some to spare. It will also be delicious on its own and quite welcome when you need a boost of healthy energy in the middle of the day.

Nonstick cooking spray

½ cup (120 ml) pure maple syrup

¾ cup (180 ml) thawed apple juice concentrate or apple cider

¼ cup (60 ml) neutral-flavored oil

60 g (¼ cup) unsweetened applesauce

280 g (2 cups) whole spelt flour

16 g (2 tablespoons) cornstarch

80 g (½ cup) packed chopped dried apple

2 teaspoons baking powder

2 teaspoons ground cinnamon

½ teaspoon fine sea salt

Preheat the oven to 350°F (180°C, or gas mark 4). Generously coat an 8 x 4-inch (20 x 10 cm) loaf pan with cooking spray.

Combine the syrup, apple juice, oil, and applesauce in a medium-size bowl.

In a large bowl, combine the flour, cornstarch, dried apple, baking powder, cinnamon, and salt.

Pour the wet ingredients onto the dry, and stir until just combined, being careful not to overmix.

Scrape the batter into the prepared pan and bake for 45 minutes, loosely covering the loaf with foil after 25 minutes (because it will brown up more quickly on top before it is done baking in the center), until a toothpick inserted into the center comes out clean.

Carefully remove the loaf from the pan and let cool completely on a wire rack before slicing.

Yield: 1 loaf

Recipe Note

We recommend using dried apples that are still somewhat soft, not crispy or overly chewy.

Whole Wheat Luau Loaf

The whole wheat pastry flour we've used in this glammed-up, super-flavorful coconut bread is ground from soft white wheat berries that retain their bran, germ, and endosperm, which are their healthiest elements. We've named the loaf in honor of Mac, a little vegan dude from Canada, who loved it a lot and said it'd be perfect for a luau. Out of the mouths of babes.

● ●

Nonstick cooking spray

80 g (1 cup) shredded unsweetened coconut

144 g (¾ cup) Sucanat

¼ cup (60 ml) neutral-flavored oil

1¼ cups (295 ml) fresh orange juice

4 ounces (113 g) mashed banana (about ½ large banana, see Note)

½ teaspoon fine sea salt

300 g (2½ cups) whole wheat pastry flour

12 g (1 tablespoon) baking powder

Preheat the oven to 350°F (180°C, or gas mark 4). Lightly coat an 8 x 4-inch (20 x 10 cm) loaf pan with cooking spray.

Combine the coconut, Sucanat, oil, orange juice, mashed banana, and salt in a large bowl. Add the flour and baking powder on top, and stir until just combined.

Scrape into the prepared pan and bake for 60 minutes, loosely covering the loaf with foil if it browns up more quickly on top before it is done baking in the center, until a toothpick inserted into the center comes out clean.

Place on a wire rack, still in the pan, for about 15 minutes before transferring directly to the rack. Let cool before slicing. Store in an airtight container or wrap in foil when completely cooled.

Yield: 1 loaf

Recipe Note

We like to freeze our bananas when they're just ripe, not black, then thaw them out by weight when ready to bake. It imparts extra moisture and flavor (whenever it's desired) just as much as if you had waited to use a super overripe (and therefore slightly icky) banana without freezing it. It works particularly well in the luau pan. Weigh 4 ounces (114 g) of frozen banana, warm in the microwave for 1 minute (or let it thaw at room temperature for 1 hour), then mash it like you mean it.

Hearty Barley Fruit Bread

This bread is an old family favorite, inspired by a recipe in a Swiss cookbook called *Le Livre du Beurre* (*The Butter Book*). We're calling it bread because it isn't a fluffy, ladylike teacake. It's more like a granola bar made into a sturdy bread, packed with loads of fiber from the dried fruits and barley flour, making it especially ideal to take along for a hike or simply to munch on when in need of a seriously delicious energy boost.

Nonstick cooking spray

96 g (½ cup) Sucanat

149 g (1 cup) dried figs, chopped

80 g (½ cup) raisins

3 ounces (85 g) diced candied orange peel

120 g (1 cup) walnuts, coarsely chopped

½ teaspoon fine sea salt

1 teaspoon ground cinnamon

Heaping ¼ teaspoon grated nutmeg

210 g (1¾ cups) barley flour

16 g (2 tablespoons) arrowroot powder or cornstarch

2 teaspoons baking powder

1 cup (235 ml) vegan milk

120 g (½ cup) plain or vanilla-flavored vegan yogurt

Preheat the oven to 350°F (180°C, or gas mark 4). Lightly coat an 8 x 4-inch (20 x 10 cm) loaf pan with cooking spray.

In a large bowl, combine the Sucanat, figs, raisins, orange peel, walnuts, salt, cinnamon, nutmeg, flour, arrowroot powder or cornstarch, and baking powder.

In a medium-size bowl, whisk together the milk and yogurt.

Pour the wet ingredients onto the dry, and stir until combined. Scrape into the prepared pan and bake for 50 minutes, until golden brown and firm on top.

Carefully remove from the pan and place on a wire rack. Let cool completely before slicing. This bread will keep well for at least a week, tightly wrapped in foil. It also freezes well.

Yield: 1 loaf

Recipe Note

A lot of store-bought candied orange peel contains high-fructose corn syrup, which is why we recommend you be on the lookout for a more natural kind when you shop for groceries or even make your own with healthier sweeteners and organic oranges so that the peel is safe to eat and pesticide-free.

Granola Teacake

Let's hope you heeded our advice and kept some of the *Coconut Spice Granola* around to make this teacake, in which we've paired oat and spelt flours to obtain a baked good that has both a light crumb and a soft texture. The granola adds a nice crunchy surprise in every bite, and its spices really shine through. Try it toasted for breakfast with a little nut butter on top.

• •

Nonstick cooking spray

1 tablespoon (15 ml) apple cider vinegar

1 cup (235 ml) vegan milk

120 g (½ cup plus 2 tablespoons) Sucanat

2 tablespoons (30 ml) neutral-flavored oil

½ cup (113 g) unsweetened applesauce

1½ teaspoons pure vanilla extract

8 g (1 tablespoon) cornstarch

90 g (1 cup) oat flour

140 g (1 cup) whole spelt flour

165 g (1½ cups) Coconut Spice Granola (page 24)

1½ teaspoons baking powder

½ teaspoon baking soda

Preheat the oven to 350°F (180°C, or gas mark 4). Lightly coat an 8 x 4-inch (20 x 10 cm) loaf pan with cooking spray.

Combine the vinegar and milk in a large bowl and let stand for 5 minutes. It will curdle and become like buttermilk.

Whisk the Sucanat, oil, applesauce, vanilla, and cornstarch into the curdled milk.

In a medium-size bowl, combine the flours, granola, baking powder, and baking soda.

Add the dry ingredients to the wet, stirring until just combined.

Scrape batter into the prepared pan and bake for 50 minutes, or until a toothpick inserted into the center of the cake comes out clean. Loosely cover with foil after 30 minutes if the cake browns too quickly.

Carefully remove cake from the pan, and let cool on a wire rack before slicing.

Yield: 1 loaf

Garam Masala Wheat and Barley Muffins

When we first saw recipes popping up online pairing sweet food items with garam masala we were a bit dubious too, so we won't blame you if you have your doubts on this one. But you are bound to be pleasantly surprised by the incredible muffins that will come out of your oven, moist from the barley flour and sweet potato purée, warm from the spices, and simply perfect to enjoy with a hot cup of tea.

• •

15 ounces (1 can, or 425 g) sweet potato purée

¼ cup (60 ml) neutral-flavored oil

2 teaspoons garam masala

144 g (¾ cup) Sucanat

16 g (2 tablespoons) cornstarch

80 g (½ cup) raisins

120 g (1 cup) whole wheat pastry flour

80 g (⅔ cup) barley flour

1 teaspoon baking powder

½ teaspoon baking soda

½ teaspoon fine sea salt

Preheat the oven to 350°F (180°C, or gas mark 4). Line a standard muffin pan with paper liners.

In a large bowl, combine the sweet potato purée, oil, garam masala, Sucanat, cornstarch, and raisins.

Combine the flours, baking powder, baking soda, and salt in a medium-size bowl. Add the dry ingredients to the wet ingredients and stir until combined.

Divide the batter among the paper liners, filling the cups three-fourths of the way full, and bake for 27 minutes or until a toothpick inserted into the center comes out clean.

Transfer to a wire rack and let cool completely. Store leftovers in an airtight container in the refrigerator for up to 4 days.

Yield: 12 muffins

Recipe Note

Those who prefer their muffins to be moderately sweet might want to use only ½ cup (96 g) Sucanat here, although our testers and ourselves found these to be just right as is. You be the judge.

Blackberry Allspice Muffins

These muffins have a lightly sweet taste and are slightly lower in fat than most muffins, thanks to the applesauce filling the role of oil. Tapioca flour acts as a binder here. Like some whole grain quick breads, they aren't high risers, but they taste wonderful. One bite and you'll be convinced that blackberries and allspice should be lifelong friends.

• •

Nonstick cooking spray

210 g (1¾ cups) whole wheat pastry flour

45 g (½ cup) oat flour

18 g (2 tablespoons) whole spelt flour

8 g (1 tablespoon) tapioca flour

12 g (1 tablespoon) baking powder

1½ teaspoons ground allspice

½ teaspoon fine sea salt

½ teaspoon baking soda

1 cup (235 ml) vegan milk

1 tablespoon (15 ml) apple cider vinegar

1 teaspoon pure vanilla extract

3 tablespoons (45 ml) neutral-flavored oil

80 g (⅓ cup) unsweetened applesauce

64 g (⅓ cup) Sucanat (see Note)

170 g (1 cup) fresh or frozen blackberries

Preheat the oven to 375°F (190°C, or gas mark 5). Coat a standard muffin pan with cooking spray.

Whisk together the flours, baking powder, allspice, salt, and baking soda in a medium-size bowl.

Combine the milk and vinegar in a medium-size bowl; the mixture will curdle and become like buttermilk. Whisk in the vanilla, oil, applesauce, and Sucanat.

Pour the wet ingredients into the dry ingredients and stir together. Stir until no flour is visible, but do not overmix. Gently fold in the berries. Spoon ⅓ cup (70 g) batter into each muffin cup.

Bake for 20 to 22 minutes, or until golden. Let cool in the pan for 5 minutes, then transfer the muffins to a wire rack to cool.

Yield: 12 muffins

Recipe Note

If you prefer sweeter muffins, add an extra 12 g (1 tablespoon) Sucanat.

Hidden Treasure Muffins

These delectable lemon muffins have a jammy surprise inside and a sweet oat topping. Whole wheat pastry flour is combined with oat flour to give it a naturally sweet edge and a beautiful crumb. Start your day off with one of these, or have one beside a salad for lunch, with a cup of tea, for an after dinner treat...any time!

● ●

Nonstick cooking spray

FOR TOPPING:

48 g (¼ cup) Sucanat

¼ teaspoon cornstarch

1 teaspoon lemon zest

10 g (2 tablespoons) quick-cooking oats

FOR MUFFINS:

240 g (2 cups) whole wheat pastry flour

90 g (1 cup) oat flour

32 g (¼ cup) cornstarch

12 g (1 tablespoon) baking powder

½ teaspoon fine sea salt

½ cup (120 ml) refrigerated coconut milk

80 g (½ cup) coconut sugar

96 g (½ cup) Sucanat

⅓ cup plus 1 tablespoon (90 ml) neutral-flavored oil

¼ cup (60 ml) fresh lemon juice

45 g (3 tablespoons) plain vegan yogurt

8 g (1 tablespoon plus 1 teaspoon) lemon zest

1 tablespoon plus 1 teaspoon (20 ml) lemon extract

80 g (¼ cup) all-fruit preserves of choice, divided

Preheat the oven to 375°F (190°C, or gas mark 5). Lightly coat a standard muffin pan with cooking spray.

TO MAKE THE TOPPING: Combine the Sucanat and cornstarch in a small blender. Blend until powdered. Let sit with the lid on for the dust to settle. Stir in the zest and oats. Set aside.

TO MAKE THE MUFFINS: Whisk together the flours, cornstarch, baking powder, and salt in a medium-size bowl.

Whisk together the milk, sugars, oil, lemon juice, yogurt, zest, and lemon extract in a medium-size bowl. Pour the wet ingredients into the dry ingredients and gently mix together. Do not overmix. Spoon 3 tablespoons (60 g) batter into each of the cups. Top each with 1 teaspoon preserves, in the very center of the muffin. Top each with 1 tablespoon (20 g) of the remaining batter, covering the preserves completely. Divide the topping equally among the muffins, about 2 teaspoons per muffin. Bake for 20 to 25 minutes, until lightly browned. Let cool for 15 minutes in the muffin pan, then transfer to a wire rack to cool completely.

Yield: 12 muffins

Whole Wheat Raisin Bran Muffins

These are a lighter, fluffier version of the classic fiber-enhanced combo that will knock everyone's socks off, including those who usually run away (while screaming like banshees, for an extra pinch of melodrama) from bran-based goods.

• •

1 tablespoon (15 ml) fresh lemon juice

15 tablespoons (220 ml) vegan milk

60 g (¼ cup) unsweetened applesauce

120 g (½ cup plus 2 tablespoons) Sucanat

2 tablespoons (30 ml) neutral-flavored oil

1½ teaspoons pure vanilla extract

180 g (1½ cups) whole wheat pastry flour

94 g (1 cup) oat bran

1 teaspoon ground cinnamon or pumpkin pie spice mix

1½ teaspoons baking powder

½ teaspoon baking soda

½ teaspoon fine sea salt

90 g (½ cup) packed raisins

Preheat the oven to 400°F (200°C, or gas mark 6). Line a standard muffin pan with paper liners.

Place the lemon juice in a 1-cup (235 ml) measure. Top with the milk. Let stand for a few minutes; it will curdle and become like buttermilk.

Transfer the milk mixture to a large bowl, add the applesauce, Sucanat, oil, and vanilla, and whisk to combine.

In a medium-size bowl, combine the flour, oat bran, cinnamon or pumpkin pie spice, baking powder, baking soda, salt, and raisins.

Add the wet ingredients to the dry, stirring until just combined.

Fill the paper liners three-fourths full and bake for 16 to 18 minutes, or until firm on top and golden brown.

Transfer the muffins to a cooling rack. Store leftovers in an airtight container in the refrigerator for up to 4 days.

Yield: 12 muffins

Peanut and Banana Whole Wheat Muffins

If you're all about big muffin tops, and a fan of anything banana paired with peanut flavor, we're ready to wager that these oh-so-tender, tall, and airy muffins will hit the spot for you. We love to use frozen bananas that are thawed before mixing the batter because they bring a little extra moisture to baked goods.

90 g (¾ cup) roasted peanut flour (see Note)

250 g (1⅔ cups) frozen banana slices, thawed

2 teaspoons pure vanilla extract

¼ cup (60 ml) neutral-flavored oil

¾ cup (180 ml) vegan milk

144 g (¾ cup) Sucanat

180 g (1½ cups) whole wheat pastry flour

16 g (2 tablespoons) cornstarch

2 teaspoons baking powder

½ teaspoon fine sea salt

80 g (⅔ cup) date crumbles (optional; see Note, page 29)

40 g (10 teaspoons) organic turbinado sugar, for sprinkling on tops (optional)

Preheat the oven to 350°F (180°C, or gas mark 4). Line a standard muffin pan with 10 paper liners. Fill the remaining 2 cups halfway with water to ensure even baking and to avoid warping the pan.

Whisk the peanut flour, thawed banana slices, vanilla, oil, milk, and Sucanat in a large bowl until mostly smooth. (You may need to mash the bananas with a fork first to make them mushy, almost liquidy.)

Sift the flour, cornstarch, baking powder, and salt into a medium-size bowl. Stir the date crumbles into the flour mixture. Stir the dry ingredients into the wet until combined.

Divide the batter equally among the 10 paper liners, and fill to the top of each liner. The muffins won't overflow because the batter is rather thick, but if you're concerned, make one or two extra muffins instead. In that case, you will want to check for doneness after 24 minutes of baking time.

Sprinkle each muffin evenly with 1 teaspoon of the turbinado sugar.

Bake for 28 minutes, or until a toothpick inserted into the center comes out clean. Carefully transfer to a wire rack to cool.

Store completely cooled leftovers in an airtight container at room temperature.

Yield: 10 to 12 muffins

Recipe Note

If you cannot find peanut flour or don't want to make your own, replace it with 120 g (1 cup) almond meal or 112 g (1 cup) hazelnut meal. You might get an extra muffin or two if you do this switch.

Coconut Zucchini Muffins

Have you had it with the ubiquitous bowl of cold cereal with a splash of vegan milk for breakfast? We've so been there. Instead, put the big bunch of zucchini you either bought at the market or grew in your own garden (lucky you) to good use by making yourself a bunch of soft, light, not overly sweet, perfect-for-breakfast muffins. These have a bit of lemon and lime zests for a refreshing flavor and shredded coconut for added texture.

• •

120 g (½ cup) plain or vanilla-flavored vegan yogurt

¼ cup (60 ml) neutral-flavored oil

¼ cup (60 ml) vegan milk

96 g (½ cup) Sucanat

98 g (1 cup) finely grated zucchini (about 1 medium zucchini)

2 teaspoons lemon zest

1 teaspoon lime zest

40 g (½ cup) unsweetened shredded coconut

1 teaspoon pure vanilla extract

180 g (1½ cups) whole wheat pastry flour

1½ teaspoons baking powder

½ teaspoon fine sea salt

Preheat the oven to 350°F (180°C, or gas mark 4). Line a standard muffin pan with 10 paper liners. Fill the remaining 2 cups halfway with water to ensure even baking and to avoid warping the pan.

Combine the yogurt, oil, milk, Sucanat, zucchini, zests, coconut, and vanilla in a large bowl.

Sift the flour, baking powder, and salt into a medium-size bowl. Stir the dry ingredients into the wet until combined.

Divide the batter equally among the 10 paper liners, filling them about two-thirds full.

Bake for 30 minutes, or until a toothpick inserted into the center comes out clean. Carefully transfer to a wire rack to cool completely.

Yield: 10 muffins

Chapter 4

Taming the Wild Yeast Beast

Knead some good grains back into your daily bread.

Forget the puffy, nutritionally void white breads of the past and open your arms to the world of whole grain yeasted breads. It doesn't matter whether you are new to yeast or an old hand, this chapter is one you really knead. And need. (Oh yes, we did.)

Perfect Pita Bread

This versatile flatbread can cover a lot of territory. Our recipe combines spelt and wheat flours, with a bit of gluten, to make an elastic and expandable dough. Not only are the pitas easy to prepare, but you can also feel better about eating them because you can pronounce every ingredient!

● ●

1¼ cups (295 ml) lukewarm water

½ teaspoon molasses

2¼ teaspoons active dry yeast

1 tablespoon (15 ml) olive oil

210 g (1½ cups) whole spelt flour

180 g (1½ cups) white whole wheat flour

18 g (2 tablespoons) vital wheat gluten

1 teaspoon fine sea salt

Canola oil, for the bowl

Combine the water, molasses, and yeast in the mixing bowl of a stand mixer fitted with a dough hook. Stir to combine and let sit 5 minutes for the yeast to activate. Add the oil, flours, gluten, and salt. Knead the bread for 5 minutes, or until smooth and elastic, adding an extra 1 tablespoon (15 ml) water or (8 g) white whole wheat flour if needed to make a cohesive dough. The dough should be smooth and slightly tacky but not sticky. Form the dough into a ball. Alternatively, the dough may be kneaded by hand for 8 minutes on a lightly floured surface.

Lightly oil a medium-size bowl. Put the dough in the bowl and turn it over so the oiled side is facing up. Cover with a clean kitchen towel and let rise in a warm place until doubled in size, 1 to 1½ hours.

Preheat the oven to 475°F (240°C, or gas mark 9). Put a large baking sheet in the oven upside down. Make sure the oven is at the proper temperature, or the pitas may not puff.

Place the dough on a lightly floured surface and deflate, pressing the dough into a round. Cut into 6 even pieces. Shape into balls and cover with a clean kitchen towel. Let rest for 30 minutes.

With a rolling pin, evenly roll out the pitas to 7 to 8-inch (17.5 to 20 cm) rounds, about ⅛-inch (3 mm) thick. Bake the pitas on the inverted baking sheet (in batches, if necessary) for 4 to 5 minutes, until puffed and the bottoms are lightly browned. Adjust the oven temperature if needed. The pitas may rip if the oven is too hot, or not rise if it is too cool. If the pitas are crackerlike, they are rolled too thin. If the pitas don't rise while baking, increase the temperature and bake them again, if it is within 10 minutes. Remove the pitas from the oven and cool on a wire rack. Store in an airtight container at room temperature for up to 4 days.

Yield: Six 8-inch (20 cm) pitas

Pretty and Wheaty Pretzels

Every time we hear the word *pretzel*, we flash back to the *Seinfeld* episode and its famous "These pretzels are making me thirsty!" line. The good news is, we don't think these chewy and tender pretzels made any of our testers too thirsty, but they sure made them satisfyingly full. "These pretzels are making me satisfyingly full!" doesn't quite have the same ring to it, though. Best news of all is, you won't even be able to tell they're made of whole grains, thanks to the lightly colored, mild-tasting, white whole wheat flour used here.

● ●

14 ounces (414 ml) canned light
   coconut milk, lukewarm

2 teaspoons pure maple syrup

2¼ teaspoons active dry yeast

480 g (4 cups) white whole wheat flour,
   more if needed

1 teaspoon fine sea salt

8 cups (2 L) water

110 g (½ cup) baking soda

Nonstick cooking spray

Pretzel salt, for sprinkling on top

Combine the coconut milk, maple syrup, and yeast in a bowl. Let sit for 5 minutes for the yeast to activate. Combine the flour and salt in a large bowl. Add the wet ingredients to the dry and stir to combine.

Turn dough out onto a lightly floured surface and knead for about 8 minutes, until the dough is smooth and pliable, adding extra flour, 1 tablespoon (8 g) at a time, if the dough is too wet. Shape into a ball. Alternatively, use a stand mixer fitted with a dough hook, and let it knead for about 6 minutes, adding extra flour, 1 tablespoon (8 g) at a time, if the dough is too wet.

Cover tightly with plastic wrap, and let rise in a warm place until doubled in size, 1 to 1½ hours.

Preheat the oven to 425°F (220°C, or gas mark 7). Line 2 large baking sheets with parchment paper or silicone baking mats.

Bring the water and baking soda to a boil in a large saucepan.

Punch down the dough. Divide it into 8 equal portions. Roll out each portion into a 22-inch (56 cm) rope. Shape the rope into a U. Hold the ends of the rope and cross them over each other, pressing them onto the bottom of the U to form a traditional pretzel shape. Place on the prepared baking sheets.

Lower the heat of the boiling water to a gentle boil. Add the pretzels one at a time and simmer for 30 seconds, submerging them occasionally. Scoop out the pretzels with a slotted spoon. Place back on the prepared baking sheets. Repeat until all have been boiled.

Lightly coat each pretzel with cooking spray and sprinkle with just enough pretzel salt to lightly cover the tops.

Bake for 12 to 14 minutes, until the pretzels are dark golden brown. Transfer to a wire rack to cool. These are best enjoyed warm, so reheat them in your toaster or oven if you eat them later. Store in an airtight container at room temperature for up to 2 days.

Yield: 8 pretzels

Cinnamon Raisin Rye Bagels

First-time bagel-maker? Fret not. Bagels are easier to make than one would think, cross our hearts. The combination of white whole wheat, dark rye, and whole spelt flours yields a hearty yet tender and, of course, traditionally chewy bagel packed with nutrition. These are very lightly sweetened with apple juice, cinnamon, and raisins.

• •

1 scant cup (220 ml) apple juice, lukewarm

2 teaspoons Sucanat

2¼ teaspoons active dry yeast

240 g (2 cups) white whole wheat flour

60 g (½ cup) dark rye flour

70 g (½ cup) whole spelt flour

1½ teaspoons ground cinnamon

1 teaspoon fine sea salt

2 tablespoons (30 ml) neutral-flavored oil

60 g (¼ cup plus 2 tablespoons) raisins

8 cups (2 L) water

55 g (¼ cup) baking soda

Combine the juice, Sucanat, and yeast in a bowl. Let sit for 5 minutes for the yeast to activate.

Combine the flours, cinnamon, and salt in the bowl of a stand mixer fitted with a dough hook. Add the oil, raisins, and yeast mixture on top of the dry ingredients. Knead for 6 minutes, adding extra whole wheat flour, 1 tablespoon (8 g) at a time, if the dough is too wet. The dough should be smooth and pliable. Alternatively, you can stir the ingredients, transfer the dough to a lightly floured surface, knead for about 8 minutes, until the dough is smooth and pliable, adding extra whole wheat flour, 1 tablespoon (8 g) at a time, if the dough is too wet. Shape into a ball.

Place in a bowl, cover tightly with plastic wrap, and let rise in a warm place until doubled in size, 1 to 1½ hours.

Line a baking sheet with parchment paper or a silicone baking mat.

Punch down the dough. Divide it into 6 equal portions and roll into circles. If the dough retracts when you try to shape it, give it 5 minutes to rest until it cooperates. Use your thumb to puncture a 1-inch (2.5 cm) hole in the center. Place on the prepared baking sheet.

Bring the water and baking soda to a boil in a large saucepan.

Preheat the oven to 400°F (200°C, or gas mark 6).

Lower the heat of the boiling water to a gentle boil. Add 2 bagels at a time and simmer for 1 minute, flipping each bagel halfway through. Scoop out the bagels with a slotted spoon. Place on the prepared baking sheet. Repeat until all the bagels have been boiled.

Transfer to the oven and bake for 14 minutes, or until the bagels are a deep golden brown and sound hollow when the bottom is tapped. Let cool on a wire rack.

Yield: 6 bagels

Pizzeria-Style Pizza Crust

If you haven't noticed, white whole wheat and spelt are truly a dynamic duo: The spelt downplays the heartiness of wheat, yielding a perfectly chewy crust. Double the recipe, set up a topping bar, and you're ready for a pizza party. Please note: The baking times are approximate. The timing will depend on the toppings, so be sure to check the pizzas as they bake.

• •

1 cup (235 ml) lukewarm water

½ teaspoon Sucanat or other sweetener

1 teaspoon active dry yeast

240 g (2 cups) white whole wheat flour

105 g (¾ cup) whole spelt flour

18 g (2 tablespoons) vital wheat gluten

2 tablespoons (30 ml) olive oil

1 teaspoon fine sea salt

Nonstick cooking spray

Pizza toppings, as desired

Stir together the water, Sucanat, and yeast in the mixing bowl of a stand mixer fitted with a dough hook. Let sit for 5 minutes for the yeast to activate. Add the flours, gluten, oil, and salt. Knead until smooth, about 5 to 6 minutes. Add an extra 1 tablespoon (15 ml) water or (8 g) white whole wheat flour if needed to make a cohesive dough. The dough should clear the sides of the bowl and adhere to the dough hook. Alternatively, the dough may be kneaded by hand on a lightly floured surface.

Lightly coat a large bowl with cooking spray. Scrape the dough into the bowl. Cover tightly with plastic wrap and let rise at room temperature for 2 hours, then put the dough in the refrigerator for 3 to 4 days. Let the dough come to room temperature for 2 hours before shaping.

Put a pizza stone, perforated metal baking round, or an inverted baking sheet in the oven. Preheat the oven to its hottest temperature. Turn the oven to broil for 5 minutes before baking, and return it to bake.

Divide the dough in half on a lightly floured piece of parchment paper. With your hands, pat and stretch the dough out to about a 10-inch (25 cm) round. Without squeezing the edges of the dough, create a rim by pushing outward from the center of the dough with your fingertips. If the dough resists, let it sit for a few minutes, then try again. Top as desired, leaving about 1 inch (2.5 cm) of the edge bare. Transfer the pizza (on the paper) to the baking stone or sheet. Bake until the edges and bottom are lightly browned, 5 to 10 minutes.

Yield: 2 pizzas

Recipe Note

The dough may be baked after refrigerating overnight, but for the best flavor and lightest texture, let the dough ripen until the third day.

Mushroom and Arugula Pie

This simple-looking pie reveals its savory secret when it's cut. Stuffed with seasoned mushrooms and healthy, peppery greens, this can be an appetizer, a lunch, or a make-and-take meal. For the best flavor, use a variety of mushrooms. Wild mushrooms are particularly good here.

• •

2 teaspoons olive oil, divided

80 g (½ cup) minced shallot

280 g (4 cups) sliced mixed mushrooms of choice

60 g (3 cups) baby arugula

2 cloves garlic, minced

¼ teaspoon dried thyme

5 g (2 tablespoons) minced fresh basil

1 teaspoon freshly squeezed lemon juice

½ teaspoon Dijon mustard

Generous pinch of fine sea salt

Generous pinch of ground black pepper

Nonstick cooking spray

1 recipe Pizzeria-Style Pizza Crust (page 82)

½ teaspoon coarse salt (optional)

Heat 1 teaspoon of the oil in a large skillet over medium heat. Add the shallot, mushrooms, arugula, garlic, and thyme. Cook, stirring occasionally, for about 4 minutes, or until the arugula is wilted. Remove from the heat and stir in the basil, lemon juice, mustard, fine sea salt, and pepper. Let cool before using.

Lightly coat a baking sheet with cooking spray. Preheat the oven to 400°F (200°C, or gas mark 6). Divide the risen dough in half. Roll each half into a 12-inch (30 cm) round. Transfer 1 round to the baking sheet. Spread the mushroom mixture evenly over the dough, leaving a 1-inch (2.5 cm) border around the edge. Put the second round on top and pinch the edges together to seal, forming a rim. Lightly brush the pie with the remaining 1 teaspoon oil. Prick a few times with a fork to let the steam escape. Sprinkle evenly with the coarse salt.

Bake for about 25 minutes, until the bottom is browned. If not serving immediately, transfer the pie to a cooling rack. Slice into wedges and serve hot, warm, or at room temperature.

Yield: One 12-inch (30 cm) pie

Recipe Note

Many stores offer presliced gourmet blends of mushrooms. If you choose these, you will need 8 ounces (227 g) of mushrooms.

Tapenade and White Bean Buns

We highly recommend enjoying these big, soft buns dipped in a warm bowl of your favorite marinara. Pop a couple of heads of garlic in the oven the next time you roast veggies so that you can use the cloves in the dough. If you don't have roasted garlic handy, add 1 to 2 cloves of minced garlic to the filling instead. Whole spelt flour and white whole wheat flour play off each other beautifully once again, with the spelt flour keeping the crumb soft and the wheat flour giving the buns the most outstanding flavor and texture.

FOR DOUGH:

1 cup (235 ml) lukewarm water, divided

22 g (1 tablespoon) molasses

2¼ teaspoons active dry yeast

280 g (2 cups) whole spelt flour

120 g (1 cup) white whole wheat flour

1 teaspoon fine sea salt

15 cloves roasted garlic, minced (optional)

2 tablespoons (30 ml) olive oil

FOR TAPENADE:

1 can (15 ounces, or 425 g) cannellini beans, drained and rinsed

80 g (½ cup) pitted kalamata and green olives

28 g (½ cup) oil-packed sliced sun-dried tomatoes

15 g (2 tablespoons) drained capers

½ teaspoon red pepper flakes, to taste

TO MAKE THE DOUGH: Combine ½ cup (120 ml) of the water with the molasses and yeast. Let sit for 5 minutes for the yeast to activate.

Place the flours and salt in the bowl of a stand mixer fitted with a dough hook. Add the garlic, oil, remaining ½ cup (120 ml) water, and yeast mixture on top. Knead for 6 minutes, until a smooth and pliable dough is obtained. Add extra whole wheat flour, 1 tablespoon (8 g) at a time, if needed. Alternatively, knead the dough on a lightly floured surface for about 8 minutes, adding extra whole wheat flour if needed, until a smooth and pliable dough is obtained. Place the dough back into the bowl.

Cover with plastic wrap and let rise in a warm place until doubled in size, 1 to 1½ hours.

TO MAKE THE TAPENADE: Place all the ingredients in a food processor. Pulse a few times just to coarsely chop the ingredients. Set aside.

Line a large baking sheet with parchment paper or a silicone baking mat. Punch down the dough and divide it into 6 equal portions. Place on a lightly floured surface or a silicone baking mat. Roll out each portion of dough into a 6 x 7-inch (15 x 18 cm) rectangle. Divide the filling among all 6 pieces of dough, approximately ¼ cup (68 g) per bun, and place it on the lower center half of the rectangle. Fold the upper half on top of the filling, and lightly press the sides to seal the bun. Cut a small vent hole on top. Loosely cover with plastic wrap and let rest for 20 minutes, until puffed.

Preheat the oven to 375°F (190°C, or gas mark 5). Bake for 20 minutes, until the buns sound hollow when the bottoms are tapped. For shiny tops, take the buns out of the oven 5 minutes before they're ready and lightly coat the tops (away from any source of heat) with cooking spray. Place the buns back in the oven, and bake for the remaining 5 minutes.

Place on a wire rack and let cool for at least 20 minutes before eating, or enjoy at room temperature.

Yield: 6 buns

Chickpea Rabe Calzoni

Seasoned beans and rabe, a classic Italian combo, are encased in our pizza dough for a hearty, flavorful (and fiber-full!) main dish. As tasty cold as they are hot, they make impressive picnic fare, especially with a bottle of wine. In the shade of a tree, on a checkered spread, these calzoni take that "a loaf of bread, a jug of wine, and thou" to a whole new level.

Nonstick cooking spray

1 teaspoon olive oil

85 g (2 cups) 1-inch (2.5 cm) pieces broccoli rabe

120 g (¾ cup) chopped onion

75 g (½ cup) chopped bell pepper, any color

123 g (¾ cup) cooked chickpeas

2 cloves garlic, minced

1 teaspoon dried oregano

8 g (1 tablespoon) nutritional yeast

1 tablespoon (15 ml) dry white wine

½ teaspoon fine sea salt

⅛ teaspoon ground black pepper

Pinch of red pepper flakes

1 recipe Pizzeria-Style Pizza Crust (page 82), divided into 6 equal portions

195 g (¾ cup) marinara sauce, plus more for dipping

Preheat the oven to 400°F (200°C, or gas mark 6). Lightly coat 2 baking sheets with cooking spray.

Heat the oil in a large skillet over medium heat. Add the rabe, onion, and bell pepper and cook for 4 minutes, stirring occasionally. Add the chickpeas, garlic, oregano, nutritional yeast, wine, salt, pepper, and red pepper flakes. Cook, stirring occasionally, for 10 minutes. Taste and adjust the seasonings.

Roll each portion of dough into a 7-inch (18 cm) round on a lightly floured surface. Scoop ½ cup (75 g) filling onto the center of the round. Top with 2 tablespoons (32 g) marinara sauce, keeping the sauce away from the edges of the round. Fold the round closed to form a half moon. Seal the edges well by crimping with wet fingers. If it is not sealed, the filling will leak out during baking. Put the half rounds on the baking sheets. Poke each calzone with a fork twice to allow the steam to escape. Bake for 20 to 25 minutes, rotating the racks once during baking. The calzoni are done when they are lightly browned and the bottoms sound hollow when tapped with your knuckles. Serve with extra heated marinara sauce on the side for dipping.

Yield: 6 calzoni

Serving Suggestions & Variations

The broccoli rabe in the store looks as if it should have been used three days ago? No problem. Just substitute 71 g (1 cup) of 1-inch (2.5 cm) pieces of broccoli for the broccoli rabe.

Wheat 'n' Rye Sauerkraut Apple Swirls

Pumpernickel flour, a dark and intensely flavored variety of rye flour, pairs so well with tangy sauerkraut, tart apples, and spices. After filling, the swirls are a feast for the eyes, too, especially with the smoked salt accent. Try these hot, warm, or at room temperature, or even sliced in half for a surprising French toast.

• •

¼ cup (60 ml) lukewarm water

2 teaspoons active dry yeast

2 teaspoons organic turbinado sugar or organic evaporated cane juice

¾ cup (180 ml) vegan ale, at room temperature and flat

270 g (2¼ cups) white whole wheat flour, more if needed

90 g (¾ cup) pumpernickel flour

2 tablespoons (30 ml) neutral-flavored oil

15 g (1 tablespoon) Dijon mustard, plus extra for dipping

1 teaspoon fine sea salt

2 teaspoons ground coriander

1 teaspoon dried dill

Nonstick cooking spray

213 g (1½ cups) drained sauerkraut, squeezed dry

½ tart apple, peeled, cored, and diced (optional)

¼ teaspoon caraway seeds

1 teaspoon smoked salt

Stir together the water, yeast, and sugar in the bowl of a stand mixer fitted with a dough hook. Let sit for 5 minutes for the yeast to activate. Add the ale, flours, oil, mustard, salt, coriander, and dill. Knead for 5 minutes, or until a smooth and cohesive dough is formed. The dough will be soft and tacky. Add an extra 1 tablespoon (15 ml) water or (8 g) whole wheat flour if needed. Form the dough into a ball on a lightly floured surface.

Lightly coat a medium-size bowl with cooking spray. Put the dough in the bowl and turn over so the oiled side is facing up. Cover with plastic wrap and refrigerate for 8 to 24 hours. Remove the dough from the refrigerator 2 hours before baking.

Preheat the oven to 375°F (190°C, or gas mark 5).

Stir together the sauerkraut, apple, if using, and caraway seeds in a small bowl.

Line a baking sheet with parchment paper or a silicone baking mat.

Roll the dough into a 10 x 12-inch (26 x 30 cm) rectangle on a lightly floured surface. Spread the sauerkraut mixture evenly on the dough, leaving 1 inch (2.5 cm) uncovered on one of the 12-inch (30 cm) sides. Starting at the other 12-inch (30 cm) side, roll the dough into a tight tube. Using a serrated knife, cut the rolls into 6 to 8 equal pieces, about 1½ inches (7.5 cm) each.

Transfer the rolls to the baking sheet and lightly flatten. Wet your fingers with water and brush them over each roll. Sprinkle each with a bit of smoked sea salt. Cover with plastic wrap and let rise in a warm place for 30 minutes, or until puffed.

Remove the plastic wrap from the sheet and bake the rolls for 20 minutes, until golden. Cool on a wire rack and serve hot, warm, or at room temperature with extra mustard for dipping.

Yield: 6 to 8 rolls

Braided Almond Oat Bread

This is a rich and tender bread, similar to challah bread, to enjoy for breakfast, brunch, or as a late afternoon snack. The almond meal adds a nutty flavor and richness, while the oat flour brings its wholesome nutrition and soft texture into the mix. If you can resist its siren's song and let it go stale, you'll find out it's exceptional when turned into vegan French toast.

• •

¾ cup (180 ml) lukewarm plain or vanilla-flavored almond milk, divided

¼ cup (60 ml) pure maple syrup, divided

330 g (2¾ cups) white whole wheat flour, divided

2¼ teaspoons active dry yeast

90 g (1 cup) oat flour

120 g (1 cup) almond meal

½ teaspoon fine sea salt

120 g (½ cup) plain or vanilla-flavored vegan yogurt, at room temperature

¼ cup (60 ml) melted coconut oil or neutral-flavored oil

Pure maple syrup or raw agave nectar, for brushing

Chopped roasted almonds, for sprinkling

Combine ½ cup (120 ml) of the milk with 1 tablespoon (15 ml) maple syrup, 60 g (½ cup) of the wheat flour, and the yeast. Let this mixture sit for 10 minutes, until bubbly.

In a large bowl, combine 240 g (2 cups) of the wheat flour and the oat flour, almond meal, and salt.

Combine the remaining ¼ cup (60 ml) milk, remaining 3 tablespoons (45 ml) maple syrup, yogurt, and oil. Pour the wet ingredients onto the dry and mix, adding the remaining ¼ cup (30 g) flour, 1 tablespoon (8 g) at a time, if needed, until the dough is smooth and pliable, about 6 minutes.

Alternatively, knead the dough by hand on a lightly floured surface for about 8 minutes, adding extra whole wheat flour if needed, until smooth and pliable.

Shape into a ball and cover with plastic wrap. Let rise in a warm place until doubled in size, 1 to 1½ hours.

Line a baking sheet with parchment paper or a silicone baking mat.

Punch down the dough, and place it on a clean surface. Divide it into 2 equal portions. Divide each portion into 3 equal portions. Roll each portion out into a 12-inch (30 cm) strand. Place 3 strands side by side, pinch them together at the top to seal, and tuck the top under slightly. Braid the strands. Pinch together and tuck the bottom of the braid as well, gently grabbing both ends of the braid and pushing together to make a neat and tight braid. Repeat with the remaining 3 strands.

Place the breads on the prepared sheet. Cover the breads with plastic wrap and let rise for 30 minutes, until puffed.

Preheat the oven to 375°F (190°C, or gas mark 5).

Bake for 20 minutes, or until golden brown on top and dark brown on the bottom. Turn the baking sheet once halfway through to ensure an even coloring and even baking of the braids.

Lightly brush the tops with maple syrup or agave nectar once out of the oven. Sprinkle with the chopped almonds. Let cool on a wire rack. The breads taste even better the next day.

Yield: 2 small breads

Bagard

This bread is a cross between a baguette and a *bâtard* (a roundish baguette). It takes a little planning ahead, but very little hands-on effort. In fact, the less you touch this dough, the better it works. We leave the bread in the oven for 5 minutes after turning it off to create a crunchy, chewy crust. For the best taste, enjoy this bread the day it is baked.

. . . .

FOR PRE-FERMENT:

1½ cups (355 ml) lukewarm water

1 teaspoon active dry yeast

180 g (1½ cups) white whole wheat flour

70 g (½ cup) whole spelt flour

FOR DOUGH:

2 tablespoons (30 ml) lukewarm water

1 teaspoon active dry yeast

½ teaspoon raw agave nectar or other sweetener

210 g (1¾ cups) white whole wheat flour, more as needed

1½ teaspoons fine sea salt

Nonstick cooking spray

1 cup (235 ml) boiling water

TO MAKE THE PRE-FERMENT: Combine the water, yeast, and flours in the bowl of a stand mixer fitted with a paddle attachment. Mix at medium speed for 5 minutes. It should resemble a thin cake batter. Cover with plastic wrap and let sit for 2 hours at room temperature, then refrigerate for 8 to 24 hours.

TO MAKE THE DOUGH: Remove the pre-ferment from the refrigerator 1 hour before using to bring to room temperature. Stir together the water, yeast, and agave. Let sit for 5 minutes, then add to the pre-ferment along with the flour and salt. Mix with the dough hook for 5 minutes. The mixture should clear the sides and bottom of the bowl, climbing up the hook. If needed, add extra flour 1 tablespoon (8 g) at a time to make a tacky, but not sticky, dough.

Coat a medium-size bowl with cooking spray. Scrape the dough into the bowl, sprinkle with flour, and swirl to form a ball. Cover with plastic wrap and let rise in a warm place until doubled in size, 1 to 1½ hours. Cut the dough into 2 equal pieces, trying not to deflate it. Sprinkle a pizza peel or a piece of parchment paper on a baking sheet with flour. Shape each half of the dough into a 12-inch (30 cm) long loaf by pulling the ends and smoothing it with your hands. Put any seams on the underside. Coat with cooking spray, sprinkle with flour, and cover with plastic wrap and a clean kitchen towel. Let rise in a warm place for 30 minutes, or until quite puffed.

Put a baking stone or an inverted baking sheet in the oven. Put a large roasting pan on the bottom of the oven or on the lowest rack. Preheat the oven to 475°F (240°C, or gas mark 9). Using a sharp knife, cut each loaf 3 times down the center. Using a spatula if needed, carefully transfer the loaves to the stone. Quickly pour the boiling water into the roasting pan and close the oven. The water will splatter and steam, so be careful. Bake for 15 to 18 minutes, until lightly browned and the bottoms sound hollow when tapped with your knuckles. Cool slightly on a wire rack before cutting.

Yield: 2 loaves

Oatmeal Sandwich Bread

If you are among those of us who have been on the hunt for a super tender, nutty-flavored (thank you, oats and whole wheat flour!), easily sliceable loaf of bread that makes for perfect sandwiches, and that while packed with good-for-you grains, doesn't taste overly healthy, this one should make you very happy indeed.

1 cup (235 ml) water, divided

40 g (½ cup) old-fashioned rolled oats

2 teaspoons pure maple syrup, divided

2¼ teaspoons active dry yeast

300 g (2½ cups) white whole wheat flour, divided, more if needed

1 teaspoon fine sea salt

2 tablespoons (30 ml) olive oil

Nonstick cooking spray

Bring ¾ cup (180 ml) of the water to a boil in a small pan over high heat. Remove from heat. Soak the oats in the boiling water for 15 minutes, until the water is mostly absorbed and the oats are soft. Make sure the water is back to lukewarm before adding the oat mixture to the rest of the ingredients.

Heat the remaining ¼ cup (60 ml) water to lukewarm. Add 1 teaspoon of the maple syrup and the yeast. Let sit for 5 minutes for the yeast to activate.

Place 240 g (2 cups) of the flour and the salt in the bowl of a stand mixer fitted with a dough hook. Add the oat mixture, yeast mixture, oil, and remaining 1 teaspoon maple syrup and mix for 6 minutes, until the dough is smooth and pliable. Add extra flour, 1 tablespoon (8 g) at a time, if the dough is too wet and sticks to the sides of the bowl.

Alternatively, knead the dough on a lightly floured surface for 8 minutes, adding extra flour if needed, until the dough is smooth and pliable.

Place the dough in a bowl, cover with plastic wrap, and let rise in a warm place until doubled in size, 1 to 1½ hours.

Lightly coat an 8 x 4-inch (20 x 10 cm) loaf pan with cooking spray.

Punch down the dough, and press it down into the prepared pan. Cover with plastic wrap and let rise for another hour, or until doubled in size.

Preheat the oven to 375°F (190°C, or gas mark 5).

Remove the plastic wrap from the pan, and bake the bread for 30 minutes, or until golden brown and the bottom sounds hollow when tapped. For a shiny bread top, grab your oven mitts, take the loaf out of the oven 5 minutes before it's ready, and lightly coat the top of the bread (away from any source of heat) with cooking spray. Place the loaf back in the oven, and bake for the remaining 5 minutes. Remove the bread from the pan and let cool completely on a wire rack before slicing.

Yield: 1 loaf

Whole Grain Burger Buns (and Sandwich Bread!)

Hats off to our friend Kelly Cavalier for thinking of using whole spelt flour instead of all-purpose flour in Celine's recipe making this bread 100% whole grain, super soft, and even better than the original version.

• •

1 cup (235 ml) lukewarm water

2¼ teaspoons active dry yeast

22 to 44 g (1 to 2 tablespoons) molasses or barley malt syrup, to taste

210 g (1½ cups) whole spelt flour

180 g (1½ cups) whole wheat flour, more if needed

1 teaspoon fine sea salt

2 tablespoons (30 ml) neutral-flavored oil

Serving Suggestions & Variations

Make a sandwich bread out of the dough by dividing it into 3 equal portions after the first rise, placing them in an 8 x 4-inch (20 x 10 cm) loaf pan coated with nonstick cooking spray. Let rise in a warm place until doubled in size, 40 minutes. Preheat the oven to 375°F (190°C, or gas mark 5). Bake for 25 minutes, until golden brown and the bottom sounds hollow when tapped. Remove from the pan and let cool on a wire rack.

Combine the water, yeast, and molasses in a medium-size bowl. Let sit for 5 minutes for the yeast to activate. Place the flours and salt in the bowl of a stand mixer fitted with a dough hook. Add the oil and yeast mixture on top. Mix until a smooth and pliable dough forms, about 6 minutes. Add extra whole wheat flour, 1 tablespoon (8 g) at a time, if needed.

Alternatively, transfer the dough to a lightly floured surface and knead for 8 minutes, adding extra whole wheat flour, 1 tablespoon (8 g) at a time if needed, until the dough is smooth and pliable. Shape the dough into a ball, place back in the bowl, cover tightly with plastic, and let rise in a warm place until doubled in size, 1 to 1½ hours. Line a large baking sheet with parchment paper or a silicone baking mat.

Gently deflate the dough. Divide it into 6 equal portions; shape into round burger buns. Place on the prepared baking sheet. Loosely cover with plastic wrap. Let rest for 30 minutes, until puffed.

Preheat the oven to 400°F (200°C, or gas mark 6). Carefully remove the plastic wrap from the buns.

Bake for 14 minutes, or until the buns are golden brown on top and sound hollow when the bottoms are lightly tapped. Let cool on a wire rack.

Yield: 6 burger buns

Pull-Apart Cinnamon Bread

This deliciously cinnamon-y and sweet recipe works best with a stand mixer, because kneading it by hand would require using too much extra flour. Whole wheat pastry flour is ground more finely than regular whole wheat flour, but it retains the same nutrition while yielding baked goods that are just as light as if they had been made with refined, nutritionally void all-purpose flour. We love to drizzle a batch of the icing from the Lemony Spelt Scones (page 18) on top of it, using vegan milk instead of lemon juice, and adding ½ teaspoon pure vanilla extract to it, but this is entirely optional for those who might have less of a sweet tooth than we occasionally do.

● ●

FOR DOUGH:

Nonstick cooking spray

8 g (1 tablespoon) cornstarch

½ cup (120 ml) water

½ cup (120 ml) lukewarm full-fat canned coconut milk

60 g (5 tablespoons) Sucanat, divided

240 g (2 cups) whole wheat pastry flour, divided, plus more for rolling out the dough

2¼ teaspoons active dry yeast

¼ teaspoon fine sea salt

¼ cup (60 ml) melted coconut oil

1½ teaspoons pure vanilla extract

FOR CINNAMON FILLING:

96 g (½ cup) Sucanat

8 g (1 tablespoon) ground cinnamon

TO MAKE THE DOUGH: Lightly coat a 7¾ x 3¾-inch (19.5 x 9.5 cm) loaf pan with cooking spray. A regular 8 x 4-inch (20 x 10 cm) loaf pan will do the trick, too, but the loaf will be slightly flatter.

Place the cornstarch in a small bowl. Add 2 tablespoons (30 ml) of the water and stir to dissolve the cornstarch completely. Add the remaining 6 tablespoons (90 ml) water, and bring to a boil either in the microwave (be sure to use a deep microwave-safe bowl, because the mixture has a tendency to bubble up) for 1 minute or in a small saucepan until it is slightly gelatinous and cloudy, about 1 minute. Let cool at room temperature before using.

Mix the coconut milk with 12 g (1 tablespoon) of the Sucanat, 60 g (½ cup) flour, and the yeast. Let this mixture sit for 10 minutes, until bubbly.

Place the remaining 180 g (1½ cups) flour in the bowl of a stand mixer, along with the remaining 48 g (¼ cup) Sucanat and the salt. Add the cornstarch mixture, yeast mixture, oil, and vanilla.

Mix on medium-high speed for 5 minutes, stopping once or twice to scrape the sides of the bowl with a rubber spatula, to make sure everything gets mixed in. The dough will look like batter even when it is done mixing. Gather it in the center of the bowl with a rubber spatula, tightly cover the bowl with a lid or plastic wrap, and let stand for 45 minutes. There won't be much of a rise; this is mostly to ensure the dough gets moistened.

Use a rubber spatula to gently deflate the sticky dough, and gather it in the center of the bowl again.

Tightly cover with plastic wrap again and refrigerate for about 1½ hours, just until the dough is stiff enough to handle easily, but not too solid because of the coconut oil. If the dough is still too soft after this time, place it back in the refrigerator and wait until it is ready; otherwise, it will be harder to handle.

TO MAKE THE FILLING: Combine the sugar and cinnamon in a bowl. Set aside.

Punch down the dough. Generously sprinkle the counter with flour. Lightly flour the dough itself, and roll it out into an approximately 8 x 12-inch (20 x 30 cm) rectangle.

Lightly brush the whole surface with water. Evenly sprinkle the cinnamon sugar on top, pressing down gently. It will look like a lot, but go for it.

Using a sharp knife, cut the rolled-out dough lengthwise into four 2-inch-wide (5 cm) strips. Place the strips on top of each other, with the sugared side facing up. Cut into 6 stacks, each one made of 4 layers.

Transfer the stacks carefully into the prepared pan. Arrange the stacks cut edges up, so it looks like stripes. Don't worry if some sugar lands on the bottom of the pan. Be sure to hold the stacks already placed in the pan up with one hand as you add the remaining ones with the other hand.

Cover with a piece of plastic wrap, and let rise in a warm place until doubled in size, 1 to 1½ hours. If you see there is not much movement after 1 hour, turn on your oven to its lowest setting, turn it off after 20 seconds, place the covered loaf in the oven, and close the door.

Remove the loaf from the oven once it has doubled in size and preheat the oven to 350°F (180°C, or gas mark 4). Line the oven rack with a piece of foil, in case of sugar spillage. Carefully remove the plastic wrap from the risen dough.

Bake for 35 minutes, until dark brown on top (not light brown, because the inside might still be raw).

Wait at least 20 minutes before digging in, because the filling will be hot. This loaf is best eaten the day it is baked.

Yield: 1 loaf

Recipe Note

The method for making pull-apart bread caught our attention when we saw cookbook author Flo Braker's Lemon-Scented Pull-Apart Coffee Cake recipe over at Leite's Culinaria. Joy Wilson, from the Joy the Baker blog, also made a similar cinnamon-filled bread, and it quickly became an Internet sensation. We couldn't resist getting on the bandwagon with our own version!

Potato and Walnut Wheat Bread

We find that although kneading this dough also works here, using a stand mixer is easiest to thoroughly incorporate the mashed potato into the flour, and to avoid being too generous with extra whole wheat flour, making for an incredibly soft and light loaf of bread. For a larger loaf, don't divide the dough in half after the first rise—shape it into one single loaf. Let it rise for 45 minutes, until puffed. Bake it for 30 minutes, until browned and hollow sounding when the bottom is tapped.

• •

¾ cup (180 ml) lukewarm water, divided

22 g (1 tablespoon) molasses

1 teaspoon active dry yeast

300 g (2½ cups) white whole wheat flour, more as needed

1 teaspoon fine sea salt

6 ounces (170 g) mashed potato

2 tablespoons (30 ml) neutral-flavored oil

75 g (heaping ½ cup) coarsely chopped walnuts

In a medium-size bowl, combine ¼ cup (60 ml) of the water, molasses, and yeast. Let sit for 5 minutes for the yeast to activate.

Place the flour and salt in the bowl of a stand mixer. Combine the mashed potato, remaining ½ cup (120 ml) water, and oil in a medium-size bowl, and pour on top of the flour mixture, along with the yeast mixture. Start mixing until a dough forms, about 8 minutes. Start incorporating the walnuts after 4 minutes of kneading time. Add extra flour if needed, 1 tablespoon (8 g) at a time, until the dough is smooth and pliable. Shape into a ball.

Alternatively, knead the dough on a lightly floured surface for 8 minutes, adding extra flour if needed, until the dough is smooth and pliable. Start incorporating the walnuts after 4 minutes of kneading time. Shape into a ball.

Place the dough in a large bowl, cover with plastic wrap, and let rise for 90 minutes.

Punch down the dough. Divide it into 2 equal portions. Flour your hands, and shape each into an approximately 8-inch (20 cm) loaf. Place the loaves on a baking sheet, making sure the bottom of the bread is well floured so that the bread won't stick as it rises and then bakes. Be careful not to leave too much flour on the sheet itself, because it might burn as the breads bake.

Sprinkle the top of the loaves with some flour. Loosely cover with plastic wrap, and let rise for another 30 minutes, until puffed.

Preheat the oven to 400°F (200°C, or gas mark 6).

Remove the plastic wrap from the loaves. Bake for 24 minutes, or until the loaves are deep brown in color and sound hollow when the bottoms are tapped. Let cool on a wire rack.

Yield: Two 8-inch (20 cm) loaves

English Muffin Bread

Yes, you can get nooks and crannies with whole grains! It just takes a few tricks. First, it's easiest with a very wet batter. So wet that it can really only be made in a stand mixer rather than by hand. Second, we especially suggest weighing the flours for this one to make sure not to overdo it on the flour. Third, right after mixing in the baking soda, pop this loaf in the oven.

½ cup (120 ml) lukewarm water

12 g (1 tablespoon plus 1 teaspoon) active dry yeast

2 teaspoons Sucanat or other sweetener

1½ cups (355 ml) unsweetened plain vegan milk

1 tablespoon (15 ml) apple cider vinegar

1 tablespoon (15 ml) neutral-flavored oil

240 g (2 cups) white whole wheat flour

70 g (½ cup) whole spelt flour

32 g (¼ cup) finely ground cornmeal

1 teaspoon fine sea salt

Nonstick cooking spray

2 teaspoons coarsely ground cornmeal, divided

1½ teaspoons baking soda

Combine the water, yeast, and Sucanat in the mixing bowl of a stand mixer fitted with the paddle attachment. Let sit for 5 minutes for the yeast to activate.

Whisk together the milk and vinegar in a small bowl. The mixture will curdle and become like buttermilk. Stir in the oil.

Whisk together the flours, finely ground cornmeal, and salt in a medium-size bowl.

Pour the milk mixture and the flour mixture into the yeast mixture. Beat on medium speed for 3 minutes. The consistency of the batter will resemble cake batter. Cover with a clean kitchen towel and let rise in a warm place until doubled in size, 1 to 1½ hours.

About 15 minutes before baking, preheat the oven to 375°F (190°C, or gas mark 5). Lightly coat an 8 x 4-inch (20 x 10 cm) loaf pan with cooking spray. Sprinkle 1 teaspoon of the coarsely ground cornmeal evenly in the bottom of the pan.

Put the bowl back on the stand mixer, and add the baking soda. Beat with the paddle attachment on low for 1 minute. Pour the batter into the loaf pan and sprinkle the top with the remaining 1 teaspoon cornmeal. Bake for 20 minutes. Check to see if the top is getting too dark, and if so, cover lightly with foil. Bake for 20 to 25 minutes longer, or until the loaf pulls away from the sides of the pan and the bottom sounds hollow when tapped with your knuckles. If the loaf resists coming out of the pan, return the loaf to the oven (covered with foil) for 5 more minutes. Transfer the loaf to a wire rack and let cool for 2 hours before cutting.

Yield: 1 loaf

Souper Bread Bowls

These little beauties are flavored with fresh herbs that can be customized to your taste and are surprisingly easy to make. Use the bowls for salads, hummus, and other favorite dips, too, for a fun and festive presentation. With a tender crust, the bread will hold together long after your soup has been slurped.

● ●

¼ cup (60 ml) lukewarm water

2¼ teaspoons active dry yeast

1 teaspoon barley malt syrup or other sweetener

½ cup (120 ml) unsweetened plain vegan milk, more as needed

10 g (packed ¼ cup) fresh basil leaves

15 g (packed ¼ cup) fresh parsley

24 g (¼ cup) chopped scallion

1 tablespoon (15 ml) olive oil

120 g (1 cup) white whole wheat flour, more as needed

140 g (1 cup) whole spelt flour

1 teaspoon fine sea salt

½ teaspoon ground black pepper

Nonstick cooking spray

Stir together the water, yeast, and syrup in the mixing bowl of a stand mixer fitted with a dough hook. Let sit for 5 minutes for the yeast to activate.

Combine the milk, herbs, scallion, and oil in a small blender. Process until completely smooth. Add the slurry, flours, salt, and pepper to the yeast mixture. Knead for 5 minutes, adding an extra 1 tablespoon (15 ml) milk or (8 g) white whole wheat flour as needed to make a smooth dough. The dough will be slightly sticky. Shape the dough into a ball. Coat a medium-size bowl with cooking spray. Put the dough in the bowl and turn over so the oiled side is facing up. Cover with a clean kitchen towel and let rise in a warm place until doubled in size, 1 to 1½ hours.

Preheat the oven to 375°F (190°C, or gas mark 4). Heavily coat the outsides of 4 oven-safe bowls with cooking spray. Invert the bowls and place on 2 baking sheets.

Turn the dough out onto a lightly floured surface. Deflate and divide into 4 equal pieces. Form into balls and cover with a clean kitchen towel. Let sit for 15 minutes. Roll each into a 7- to 8-inch (18 to 20 cm) round. Pat the dough onto the outside of the bowls, gently stretching it to cover the bowl. Use the bowl to shape the dough, but don't press the dough against it too hard or it may be difficult to remove. Repair any tears with wet fingers.

Bake for 20 minutes, then carefully remove the dough from the bowl, putting the dough bowl on the baking sheet right side up. Bake for 10 minutes longer, until the inside is golden. Cool on a wire rack.

Yield: 4 bread bowls

Recipe Note

The ideal bowls are Pyrex and measure 3 inches (7.5 cm) across the exterior of the bottom and 6 inches (15 cm) across the interior of the top of the bowl with angled sides.

Whole Grain Artisan Bread

Very few ingredients paired with a no-knead method (the original no-knead method being made famous by Jim Lahey, the world-renowned baker), make for a super crusty bread with an airy crumb and a chewy texture you might not expect from something whole grain. The size and depth of a stand mixer bowl is ideal to do the dough-swirling stunt to avoid seeing the ball of dough fly across the kitchen. It's a bird, it's a plane ...

- 350 g (2¾ cups plus 2 tablespoons) white whole wheat flour, more as needed
- 1 teaspoon fine sea salt
- 1 teaspoon instant yeast
- 1⅓ cups (315 ml) water, at room temperature

Place all the ingredients in a large bowl. Mix with a rubber spatula to thoroughly combine, until the flour is fully incorporated, about 1 minute. The dough should come together rather easily, so if the flour absorbs the water too quickly and the dough is impossible to combine, add extra water, 1 tablespoon (15 ml) at a time, until you can easily combine the ingredients. Cover tightly with plastic wrap, and let rise at room temperature for 4 hours.

Remove the plastic wrap, use a rubber spatula to un-stick the dough from the sides and bottom of the bowl, generously sprinkle with flour, and swirl the dough around in the flour simply by vigorously shaking the bowl, without kneading or incorporating the flour into the dough: This will wake the yeast and ensure it continues doing its job properly. Cover tightly with plastic wrap and place in the refrigerator for approximately 18 hours.

Remove the bowl from the refrigerator and leave it out for 2 hours to bring it back to room temperature.

Place a 10-inch (25 cm) or larger Dutch oven with its lid in the oven. Preheat the oven to 475°F (240°C, or gas mark 9).

Once the oven has reached the desired temperature, use a spatula to un-stick the dough from the sides and bottom of the bowl again, generously sprinkle the dough again with more flour, and vigorously shake the bowl to swirl the dough around, without kneading or incorporating the flour.

Carefully transfer to the preheated Dutch oven. Use scissors to cut ¾-inch (2 cm) slits into the top of the dough that will allow the bread to expand as it bakes. Evenly sprinkle the top with a generous amount of flour. Cover with the lid.

Bake for 20 minutes with the lid on, then remove the lid and bake for another 10 minutes. Carefully tap the bottom of the bread with your knuckles. The bread is ready once it sounds hollow and the top is deep golden brown.

Let cool on a wire rack for several hours before slicing. The bread is best enjoyed the day it is baked.

Yield: 1 loaf

Amaranth Spelt and Olive Round

Imagine yourself in the Italian countryside: warm sunshine, soft breezes, picturesque villages, a bottle of wine, and this bread. Studded with olives, this finely textured loaf can be sliced thinly and served on a vegan cheese and fruit plate. It makes fast friends with soups and salads, too.

● ●

¼ cup (60 ml) lukewarm water

2 teaspoons active dry yeast

1 teaspoon raw agave nectar or other sweetener

180 g (1½ cups) white whole wheat flour, more if needed

70 g (½ cup) whole spelt flour

30 g (¼ cup) amaranth flour

9 g (1 tablespoon) vital wheat gluten

½ teaspoon fine sea salt

¾ cup plus 2 tablespoons (210 ml) unsweetened plain vegan milk, at room temperature, divided

2 tablespoons (30 ml) olive oil

50 g (½ cup) pitted kalamata olives, chopped

Nonstick cooking spray

Stir together the water, yeast, and agave in the bowl of a stand mixer fitted with a dough hook. Let sit for 5 minutes for the yeast to activate.

Add the flours, gluten, salt, ¾ cup (180 ml) of the milk, and the oil. Knead the dough until smooth and elastic, about 5 minutes, adding the remaining 2 tablespoons (30 ml) milk 1 tablespoon (15 ml) at a time, if needed, to make a cohesive dough. Alternatively, the dough may be kneaded by hand on a lightly floured surface.

Knead the olives into the dough by hand. The olives may add moisture to the bread, so add extra white whole wheat flour, 1 tablespoon (8 g) at a time, if needed. The dough should be slightly tacky but not sticky. Form the dough into a ball.

Lightly coat a large bowl with cooking spray. Put the dough in the bowl and turn over so the oiled side is facing up. Cover with a clean kitchen towel and let rise in a warm place until doubled in size, 1 to 1½ hours.

Pat the dough down on a lightly floured surface and form into a ball again. Coat a baking sheet with cooking spray. Put the rounded dough on the sheet and cover with a clean kitchen towel and let rise in a warm place until puffed, about 45 minutes.

Place a baking stone or an inverted baking sheet in the oven. Preheat the oven to 375°F (190°C, or gas mark 5). Cut the top of the bread 2 or 3 times with a sharp knife. Bake for 20 minutes, or until the loaf sounds hollow when tapped on the bottom with your knuckles. Let cool on a wire rack. For a soft crust, lightly brush the loaf with olive oil, if desired.

Let cool on a wire rack for several hours before slicing.

Yield: 1 loaf

Cracked-Wheat Pan Rolls

Although often thought to be the same, cracked wheat and bulgur wheat are not identical. Cracked wheat is exactly what it sounds like: cracked wheat berries. Bulgur is parboiled wheat, which has the bran removed during grinding. Here, the cracked wheat brings a chewy element to these otherwise very light rolls. These picture-perfect dinner rolls have a regular spot on our holiday tables, but they are easy enough for any meal.

• •

1½ cups (355 ml) lukewarm water, divided

80 g (½ cup) coarse cracked wheat

3 tablespoons (45 ml) pure maple syrup, divided

8 g (1 tablespoon) active dry yeast

3 tablespoons (45 ml) neutral-flavored oil

240 g (2 cups) white whole wheat flour, more as needed

70 g (½ cup) whole spelt flour

27 g (3 tablespoons) vital wheat gluten

1 teaspoon fine sea salt

Nonstick cooking spray

Bring 1 cup (235 ml) of the water to a boil in a pan over high heat. Decrease the heat to low and stir in the cracked wheat. Cook, stirring occasionally, for 4 minutes. The wheat may be very thick. Let cool to room temperature, about 10 minutes.

Combine the remaining ½ cup (120 ml) water with 1 tablespoon (15 ml) of the maple syrup and the yeast in the mixing bowl of a stand mixer fitted with a dough hook. Let sit for 5 minutes for the yeast to activate. Add the cracked wheat (and any remaining liquid), the remaining 2 tablespoons (30 ml) maple syrup, oil, flours, vital wheat gluten, and salt.

Knead on low speed until the dough is smooth and elastic, about 5 minutes. If there was unabsorbed liquid, you may need to add more flour. Add extra white whole wheat flour, 1 tablespoon (8 g) at a time, or 1 tablespoon (15 ml) water, if needed, to make a soft and cohesive dough. Alternatively, the dough may be kneaded by hand on a lightly floured surface for about 10 minutes. Form the dough into a ball.

Lightly coat a medium-size bowl with cooking spray. Put the dough in the bowl and turn over so the oiled side is facing up. Cover with a clean kitchen towel. Let rise in a warm place until doubled in size, 1 to 1½ hours.

Turn the dough out onto a lightly floured surface and cut into 12 equal pieces. Roll each piece into a ball. Lightly coat a 9-inch (23 cm) square or round pan with cooking spray. Put the rolls into the pan evenly. Cover with a clean kitchen towel and let rise in a warm place until quite puffed, about 45 minutes.

While rising, preheat the oven to 375°F (190°C, or gas mark 5). Bake the rolls for 20 minutes, or until nicely browned. Serve the rolls in the pan while hot, or let cool for 30 minutes before removing the connected rolls from the pan.

Yield: 12 rolls

Sun-Dried Tomato Focaccia

The flavor of our focaccia is enhanced by starting with a sponge, which is a form of pre-ferment. In short, pre-ferment means to combine a few of the ingredients ahead of the others. This technique increases the flavor and gives the yeast a head start. Whether served as a finger food at a party or pressed into duty for a sandwich, it's a big-flavored, crispy-crusted bread that we can't stop eating. Here, we've boosted it with onion and sun-dried tomatoes to make it even more addictive.

● ●

FOR PRE-FERMENT:

1 cup (235 ml) lukewarm water

½ teaspoon Sucanat or other sweetener

1 teaspoon active dry yeast

123 g (¾ cup plus 2 tablespoons) whole spelt flour

60 g (½ cup) white whole wheat flour

30 g (¼ cup) pumpernickel flour

FOR DOUGH:

120 g (1 cup) white whole wheat flour

5 tablespoons (75 ml) olive oil, divided, more if desired

55 g (⅓ cup) finely minced onion

20 g (⅓ cup) minced sun-dried tomatoes (moist, vacuum-packed)

1 teaspoon dried rosemary

1 teaspoon fine sea salt

¼ to ½ teaspoon pretzel salt or other coarse salt

TO MAKE THE PRE-FERMENT: Combine the water, Sucanat, and yeast in the mixing bowl of a stand mixer fitted with a dough hook. Let sit for 5 minutes for the yeast to activate. Add the flours and mix for 4 minutes. Cover the bowl with plastic wrap and let sit at room temperature for 2 hours.

TO MAKE THE DOUGH: Add the white whole wheat flour, 2 tablespoons (30 ml) of the oil, onion, sun-dried tomatoes, rosemary, and sea salt to the pre-ferment and knead for 8 to 10 minutes. The dough should clear the sides of the bowl and climb up the hook. It should be slightly sticky. If needed, add an extra 1 tablespoon (15 ml) water or (8 g) flour to make a cohesive dough. Cover the bowl with plastic wrap and let rise for 2 hours at room temperature.

Transfer to the refrigerator and let rise for 12 to 24 hours.

Remove from the refrigerator and let the dough come to room temperature for 2 hours before baking.

Spread 2 tablespoons (30 ml) oil in a 9 x 12-inch (23 x 30 cm) rimmed baking sheet. Put the dough in the pan, patting it into a 7 x 9-inch (18 x 23 cm) rectangle. The dough will be sticky, so flour your hands or wet them with water to reduce sticking. Try not to flatten the bread so it will retain some airy holes. Brush with the remaining 1 tablespoon (15 ml) oil. Sprinkle with the pretzel salt. Let rise in a warm place for 1 hour. It will be slightly puffy.

Preheat the oven to 500°F (250°C, or gas mark 10). Bake for 12 to 15 minutes, until the top is golden and the bottom is slightly darkened. The focaccia cuts best when slightly cooled. Cut and serve from the pan. If the focaccia sticks to the pan, gently loosen it with a metal spatula. Serve warm or at room temperature.

Yield: 1 focaccia

Chapter 5

Smarter Snacking Sessions

Treat yourself to healthier cookies, crackers, and other snacking options.

Are you on the hunt for appetizers to bring to a party?
In need of something light to go with lunch or for some easy,
pleasing munching after school or work? Feeling as though if you
don't have a cookie now, the world will surely come to an end?
Fret not: This chapter has everything you're looking for, and then some.

Caraway, Rye, and Spelt Hearts

Part cracker, part biscuit, these savory, hearty, and heart-healthy treats are perfect with fruit and vegan cheese for a light snack or supper, or with a big bowl of vegan soup. They are called hearts because that's the shape we picked for our cookie cutter, but use any shape you have. We're just big softies.

● ●

175 g (1¼ cups) whole spelt flour

120 g (1 cup) dark rye flour

2 teaspoons baking powder

1 scant teaspoon fine sea salt, to taste

13 g (2 tablespoons) caraway or sesame seeds, or a combination

2 teaspoons onion powder

¼ cup (60 ml) neutral-flavored oil

½ cup (120 ml) water, as needed

Preheat the oven to 350°F (180°C, or gas mark 4). Line a baking sheet with parchment paper or a silicone baking mat.

Combine the flours, baking powder, salt, seeds, and onion powder in a large bowl. Pour the oil on top, and use a fork to evenly distribute it throughout the mixture.

Slowly add the water until a kneadable and soft dough is obtained. Knead a few times to make sure all the ingredients are well combined and incorporated.

Turn out the dough onto a large silicone mat and roll out to approximately ¼ inch (6 mm) thick. Use a 2-inch (5 cm) cookie cutter to cut out the crackers and transfer to the prepared sheet. Prick the top of each cracker 3 times with the tines of a fork.

Bake for 16 minutes, or until golden brown on the bottom (pick one up with oven mitts to have a look). Transfer to a wire rack to cool for 20 minutes, to let the crackers crisp up. Let cool completely before placing in an airtight container.

Enjoy within a day, two at the most, after baking.

Yield: Approximately 30 crackers

Whole Grain Wonder Crackers

These crackers are just packed with goodness: amaranth, barley, and whole wheat flours. Amaranth is one of our favorite flours (admittedly, among many) because of its distinctive flavor, which is enhanced with the buttery boost of barley flour. Amaranth is pricier than some flours, but a little bit goes a long way.

• •

90 g (¾ cup) whole wheat pastry flour

23 g (3 tablespoons) barley flour

15 g (2 tablespoons) amaranth flour

¾ teaspoon herbes de Provence

½ teaspoon onion powder

½ teaspoon fine sea salt

1 tablespoon (15 ml) olive oil

¼ cup (60 ml) water

Preheat the oven to 325°F (170°C, or gas mark 3). Line a baking sheet with parchment paper or a silicone baking mat.

Combine the flours, herbes de Provence, onion powder, and salt in a medium-size bowl. Stir together with a fork. Drizzle in the oil and stir with a fork until small beads form in some parts of the flour. Drizzle in the water and continue to stir until a soft dough forms. If necessary, add more pastry flour or water, 1 teaspoon at a time. The dough will be slightly wet but not sticky. Knead the dough a few times to make sure it's well mixed.

Turn out the dough onto a lightly floured piece of parchment paper and roll out to ¹∕₁₆-inch (1.5 mm) thick. Thinner crackers will bake more quickly and be slightly crispier than thicker crackers. Cut the crackers into 2 x 3 inch (5 x 7.5 cm) rectangles using a pizza cutter or sharp knife. Carefully lift the crackers from the rolling surface using a butter knife or very thin spatula and transfer them to the baking sheet. Bake for 18 to 23 minutes, until the edges are light brown. Transfer the crackers to a wire rack. They will continue to crisp up as they cool. The crackers can be stored in an airtight container for up to 2 weeks.

Yield: 12 crackers

Noochy Crackers

What is nooch? Legend has it that someone on the Post Punk Kitchen boards coined the term as a friendlier way to refer to nutritional yeast, the cheesy-tasting, B-complex-rich powder over which so many of us vegans go gaga. The nooch is responsible for making these crackers reminiscent of the non-vegan, fish-shaped snacks that aren't exactly the poster child for minimally processed food. Have some Noochy Crackers instead, won't you?

● ●

105 g (¾ cup) whole spelt flour

60 g (½ cup) whole wheat pastry flour

30 g (¼ cup) nutritional yeast

1 teaspoon dried cilantro or other fragrant dried herb (optional)

½ teaspoon ground black pepper

1 scant teaspoon fine sea salt, to taste

3 tablespoons (45 ml) neutral-flavored oil

6 tablespoons (90 ml) water, more if needed

Preheat the oven to 350°F (180°C, or gas mark 4). Line 2 baking sheets with parchment paper or silicone baking mats.

Combine the flours, yeast, cilantro, pepper, and salt in a medium-size bowl. Add the oil and stir, then add the water, 1 tablespoon (15 ml) at a time, and mix until a kneadable dough forms. This can be done with a stand mixer fitted with a paddle attachment, or with a fork and then by hand kneading until well combined.

Turn out the dough onto a lightly floured piece of parchment paper and roll out to ⅛- to ¼-inch (3 to 6 mm) thick. The thinner the dough, the crispier the baked crackers will be. We like ours to still have a little body to them.

Cut out shapes using the smallest cookie cutters, about 1 to 2 inches (2.5 to 5 cm) in diameter. Repeat until you run out of dough, rolling it out again between batches. Place the crackers on the prepared sheets.

Bake for 15 to 18 minutes, depending on thickness, until the crackers are light golden brown on the bottom. Baking time will depend on the size of the cutter and the thickness of the cracker. Start checking early if you are using a tiny cutter/thin cracker, and be a little more patient if using a large cutter/thicker cracker. Let cool on the sheet.

Store in an airtight container once cooled. These keep well for about a week at room temperature.

Yield: About 30 crackers, depending on the size of the cookie cutter

Garlic Naan

Best known for its role in Indian cuisine, naan deserves more recognition on the baking front. This soft, mildly spiced bread, which is topped with garlic, is a savory sensation. The barley flour rounds out the flour blend, enhancing the flavor. Besides snacking, naan is great for sandwiches.

● ●

½ cup (120 ml) lukewarm water, more as needed

1 teaspoon raw agave nectar or pure maple syrup

1 teaspoon active dry yeast

3 tablespoons (45 ml) olive oil, divided

45 g (3 tablespoons) unsweetened plain vegan yogurt

3 cloves garlic, minced, divided

180 g (1½ cups) white whole wheat flour, more as needed

35 g (¼ cup) whole spelt flour

23 g (3 tablespoons) barley flour

½ teaspoon onion powder

½ teaspoon ground coriander

½ teaspoon dried cilantro

½ teaspoon fine sea salt

Nonstick cooking spray

¼ teaspoon garlic salt

½ teaspoon black onion seeds (charnushka, optional)

Combine the water, agave nectar, and yeast in the mixing bowl of a stand mixer fitted with a dough hook. Let sit for 5 minutes for the yeast to activate.

Stir in 2 tablespoons (30 ml) of the oil, the yogurt, and 2 cloves of the garlic. Add the flours, onion powder, coriander, cilantro, and sea salt. Mix on low speed for 5 minutes, until a smooth and cohesive dough forms. The dough should be tacky, but not wet or sticky. Add an extra 1 tablespoon (15 ml) water or (8 g) white whole wheat flour as needed.

Alternatively, the dough may be kneaded by hand on a lightly floured surface. Form the dough into a ball. Coat a medium-size bowl with cooking spray. Put the dough in the bowl and turn so the oiled side is facing up. Cover with a clean kitchen towel and let rise in a warm place for 2 to 2½ hours. The dough will not quite double.

Preheat the oven to 500°F (250°C, or gas mark 10). Put a pizza stone or an inverted baking sheet in the oven.

Combine the remaining 1 tablespoon (15 ml) oil and the remaining 1 clove garlic in a small bowl. Stir in the garlic salt. Set aside.

Divide the dough into 4 pieces about 4 ounces (113 g) each. Roll into balls and let rest, covered with a clean kitchen towel, for 20 minutes. Using a rolling pin, roll each ball into an oval 4 x 6 inches (10 x 15 cm). Pat the dough with wet fingers and sprinkle evenly with the onion seeds. Bake for 3 to 4 minutes, until golden. Transfer to a wire rack and brush evenly with the reserved garlic oil.

Yield: 4 naan

Whole Grain Tortillas

When we look at the ingredients on a package of tortillas, our eyes cross. Have you seen that list? The answer? Homemade! With ingredients you can recognize, these taste far better than store-bought tortillas, too. We admit that our version isn't authentic, but we do add traditional cornmeal. We find it gives the tortillas a bit more substance but doesn't make them dense.

• •

90 g (¾ cup) white whole wheat flour, more as needed

105 g (¾ cup) whole spelt flour

70 g (½ cup) finely ground cornmeal

1 teaspoon baking powder

¾ teaspoon fine sea salt

¾ cup (180 ml) unsweetened plain vegan milk, more as needed

1 tablespoon (15 ml) neutral-flavored oil

Combine the flours, cornmeal, baking powder, and salt in a medium-size bowl. Stir together.

Combine the milk and oil in a small bowl. Stir together. Pour the milk mixture into the flour mixture and stir to combine. Add an extra 1 tablespoon (15 ml) milk or (8 g) white whole wheat flour if needed to make a cohesive dough. Your hands should not stick to the dough. Turn out the dough onto a lightly floured surface and knead for about 3 minutes, until smooth. Divide into 12 equal pieces and shape into balls. Cover with a clean kitchen towel and let rest for 30 minutes.

Using a rolling pin, roll each ball out on a lightly floured surface until it is about 6 inches (15 cm) across, or as thin as possible.

Heat a large cast-iron skillet over medium heat. Put a tortilla in the skillet and cook for 2 to 3 minutes, until the bottom is golden. If parts of the tortilla are burning, decrease the heat. Turn the tortilla over with a spatula to cook the second side, about 2 minutes, until golden. To keep warm before serving, store the tortillas between 2 plates, with the top plate inverted to hold in the moisture. Or wrap the tortillas in a clean, damp kitchen towel.

Yield: 12 tortillas

Pesto Knots

It is easy to make these beautiful knotted rolls. With basil and garlic inside and out, these are a show-stopping crowd-pleaser. You and your friends will feel as if you are in the Sicilian sunshine. They travel well, so pack them in a picnic basket for al fresco dining. We love garlic, but if you don't, or have no concerns about vampires, feel free to use less.

• •

¼ cup (60 ml) lukewarm water

1 teaspoon pure maple syrup

2¼ teaspoons active dry yeast

105 g (¾ cup) whole spelt flour, divided

33 g (packed ¾ cup plus 1 tablespoon) fresh basil leaves, divided

⅓ cup (80 ml) unsweetened plain vegan milk, more as needed

¼ cup (60 ml) olive oil, divided

9 g (1 tablespoon) pine nuts

8 g (1 tablespoon) nutritional yeast

1 tablespoon (15 ml) ume plum vinegar

5 cloves garlic, minced, divided

1 teaspoon white miso paste

½ teaspoon fine sea salt

Pinch of ground black pepper

120 g (1 cup) white whole wheat flour, more as needed

Nonstick cooking spray

Stir together the water, maple syrup, and yeast in the bowl of a stand mixer fitted with a dough hook. Let sit for 5 minutes for the yeast to activate. Mix in 35 g (¼ cup) of the spelt flour. Let sit for 30 minutes.

Combine 30 g (¾ cup) of the basil, milk, 3 tablespoons (45 ml) of the oil, pine nuts, nutritional yeast, vinegar, 3 cloves of the garlic, miso, salt, and pepper in a small blender. Process until completely smooth. Pour into the yeast mixture and add the remaining 70 g (½ cup) whole spelt flour and the whole wheat flour. Knead for 5 minutes to form a smooth and cohesive dough. Add an extra 1 tablespoon (15 ml) milk or (8 g) white whole wheat flour if needed to make a soft, slightly tacky dough. It should not be sticky. Alternatively, the dough may be kneaded by hand on a lightly floured surface. Form the dough into a ball.

Lightly coat a medium-size bowl with cooking spray and put the dough in the bowl, turning it over so the oiled side is facing up. Cover with a clean kitchen towel and let rise in a warm place until doubled in size, 2 hours.

Combine the remaining 2 cloves garlic and remaining 1 tablespoon (15 ml) oil in a small bowl.

Line a baking sheet with parchment paper or a silicone baking mat.

Deflate the dough on a lightly floured surface. Cut into 8 equal pieces. Roll each piece into a 12-inch (30 cm) rope. Tie a knot close to the center of the dough, tuck under the ends, and place on the baking sheet. Repeat with the remaining pieces. Cover with a clean kitchen towel and let rise in a warm place until doubled in size, 1 hour.

Preheat the oven to 400°F (200°C, or gas mark 6).

Remove the kitchen towel and bake the dough for 13 to 15 minutes, until the bottoms sound hollow when tapped with your knuckles.

Use a spoon to drizzle the garlic oil on the knots. Mince the remaining 3 g (1 tablespoon) basil and sprinkle over the rolls.

Yield: 8 knots

To Each His/Her Own Spelt-Crusted Quiche

The dried shiitake mushrooms impart a cozy warmth and savory flavor to the filling of these individual quiches, making it a perfect match for their oil-free, tahini-based spelt flour crust. They even received the approval of definitely-not-vegan eaters: If that isn't a great endorsment, we don't know what is.

• •

FOR CRUST:

Nonstick cooking spray

210 g (1½ cups) whole spelt flour

¼ teaspoon fine sea salt

64 g (¼ cup) tahini

¼ cup (60 ml) vegetable broth,
    more if needed

FOR FILLING:

6 g (¼ cup) packed dried shiitake
    mushrooms, rinsed if gritty

¼ cup (60 ml) warm vegetable broth

12 ounces (340 g) silken firm tofu

1 clove garlic, minced

2 teaspoons onion powder

¼ teaspoon fine sea salt

⅛ teaspoon grated nutmeg

Freshly cracked rainbow peppercorn,
    to taste

1 tablespoon (15 ml) olive oil

8 g (1 tablespoon) cornstarch

23 g (3 tablespoons) nutritional yeast

¼ teaspoon turmeric

½ teaspoon baking powder

40 g (1 cup) packed chopped kale
    (without ribs)

Preheat the oven to 375°F (190°C, or gas mark 5).

TO MAKE THE CRUST: Lightly coat six 5-inch (13 cm) wide x 1¼-inch (3 cm) deep tart pans with cooking spray.

Add the flour, salt, and tahini to a food processor. Pulse a few times to combine. Add the broth, 1 tablespoon (15 ml) at a time, until the dough is moist enough to hold together when pinched. Divide the dough equally among the 6 prepared pans, using approximately ⅓ cup (60 g) crumbled crust per quiche. Press down at the bottom and approximately ¾ inch (2 cm) up the sides, and level the edges with your fingers for a more even, cleaner look.

TO MAKE THE FILLING: Soak the mushrooms in the warm broth until tender, about 2 minutes. Do not squeeze out the liquid from the mushrooms, and reserve any of the broth that might not have been absorbed. Add the mushrooms to a food processor along with the tofu, garlic, onion powder, salt, nutmeg, pepper, oil, cornstarch, nutritional yeast, and turmeric. Process until smooth. If the preparation is too thick, add a little of the reserved mushroom soaking broth until it is more manageable: It should not be liquid, but not too dry, either. Pulse the baking powder into the preparation. Pulse the kale into the preparation, just so that it is evenly distributed throughout and no large pieces remain.

Divide the filling among the 6 crusts, spreading it evenly with an offset spatula, and bake for 25 minutes, or until the top of the filling is set and light golden brown. Place on a wire rack to cool just a few minutes before serving.

Yield: 6 individual quiches

Black Bean Taco Tart

This taco-influenced tart is layered high. So high, in fact, that we almost called it the Skyscraper. It all starts with a satisfying crust made with cornmeal, which is topped with a creamy avocado filling, and decked out with the usual taco fixings. This tart has it all: healthy grains, protein-rich black beans, crisp lettuce, juicy tomatoes, and of course, lush avocados. Adapt the toppings to suit your tastes.

FOR CRUST:

Nonstick cooking spray

7 g (1 tablespoon) flax meal

9 tablespoons (135 ml) cold water, divided

123 g (¾ cup plus 2 tablespoons) whole spelt flour

60 g (½ cup) whole wheat pastry flour

60 g (½ cup) cornmeal (any kind)

1 teaspoon dried cilantro

1¼ teaspoons fine sea salt, divided

3 tablespoons (45 ml) neutral-flavored oil

FOR FILLING:

120 g (½ cup) unsweetened plain vegan yogurt

2 or 3 chipotle chiles in adobo, minced, to taste

20 g (2 tablespoons) minced onion

2 tablespoons (30 ml) fresh lemon juice

2 cloves garlic, minced

Pinch of ground black pepper

2 avocados, peeled and pitted

115 g (⅔ cup) cooked black beans

105 g (1½ cups) shredded lettuce

90 g (½ cup) chopped tomato

12 g (2 tablespoons) minced scallion

1 g (1 tablespoon) minced fresh cilantro

58 g (¼ cup) salsa, more to taste

Preheat the oven to 400°F (200°C, or gas mark 6). Lightly coat a 9-inch (23 cm) tart pan with cooking spray.

TO MAKE THE CRUST: Stir together the flax meal and 3 tablespoons (45 ml) of the water. Set aside to thicken.

Combine the flours, cornmeal, dried cilantro, and ¾ teaspoon of the salt in a medium-size bowl. Stir together with a fork. Add the oil and stir so it looks like crumbles. Add the flax mixture and 5 tablespoons (75 ml) of the water, stirring until the dough holds together. Add the remaining 1 tablespoon (15 ml) water if needed to make a shapeable mixture. Press the dough onto the sides and bottom of the tart pan. Bake for 20 to 24 minutes, until the edges are golden. Let cool before filling.

TO MAKE THE FILLING: While the crust bakes, whisk together the yogurt, chiles, onion, lemon juice, garlic, remaining ½ teaspoon salt, and pepper. Finely mince 1 of the avocados and stir it into the mixture. Chop the remaining avocado.

Spread half of the yogurt mixture evenly in the crust. Layer the beans, lettuce, tomato, chopped avocado, scallion, and fresh cilantro on top. Dollop with the salsa and remaining half of the yogurt mixture.

Yield: One 9-inch (23 cm) tart

Recipe Note

It's easiest to pat the crust against the sides of the tart pan first, then press the remaining crust into the bottom of the tin.

Roasted Vegetable Tart

As flavorful as it is colorful, this tart is a tasty addition to an appetizer spread or with a salad for lunch. The pine nuts and chickpea and barley flours bring a complexity to the crust, as well as giving it an almost biscuitlike texture.

• •

2 red bell peppers

140 g (1 cup) whole spelt flour

15 g (2 tablespoons) barley flour

15 g (2 tablespoons) chickpea flour

35 g (¼ cup) pine nuts

1 teaspoon baking powder

½ teaspoon fine sea salt, plus more for seasoning asparagus

3 tablespoons (45 ml) olive oil, divided

¼ cup (60 ml) water

8 ounces (227 g) asparagus, cut into 5-inch (13 cm) lengths

¼ teaspoon ground black pepper

6 ounces (scant ¾ cup, or 170 g) silken extra-firm tofu

2 tablespoons (16 g) nutritional yeast

1 tablespoon (15 ml) ume plum vinegar

1 teaspoon Dijon mustard

1 teaspoon light miso

3 g (1 tablespoon) chopped fresh basil

Preheat the oven to 475°F (240°C, or gas mark 9). Put the peppers on a baking sheet and bake for 15 minutes, turning occasionally. The peppers should be blackened. Transfer the peppers to a bowl and cover with plastic wrap to steam the peppers for 15 minutes. Peel the skins from the peppers and remove the seeds. Cut into ½-inch (1.3 cm) strips. Lower the oven temperature to 400°F (200°C, or gas mark 6).

Combine the flours, pine nuts, baking powder, and salt in a food processor. Process until the pine nuts are powdered and the ingredients are mixed. While the motor is running, drizzle in 2 tablespoons (30 ml) of the oil and the water. The mixture should pack together when squeezed with your hands. Add an extra 1 teaspoon water or flour, if needed.

Transfer the mixture to a 9-inch (23 cm) tart pan. Pack the crust onto the sides and bottom of the pan. Put the pan on a baking sheet and bake for 14 minutes, until the edges are lightly browned. Let cool on the sheet on a wire rack for 30 minutes or longer.

While the crust is baking, toss the asparagus with the remaining 1 tablespoon (15 ml) oil on a baking sheet. Season with salt and pepper and bake until tender, about 10 minutes.

Combine the tofu, nutritional yeast, vinegar, mustard, and miso in a blender. Process until smooth. Spread the tofu mixture in the crust and top with the asparagus and pepper strips, alternating to create a pattern. Sprinkle with the basil and serve.

Yield: One 9-inch (23 cm) tart

Instant Gratification Injera

Before anyone else points it out, let us say it loud and clear: These are not authentic Ethiopian flatbreads, which are made from teff flour alone and require fermentation. But they can be made in a matter of minutes, taste fantastic, and are the perfect complement to curries, soups, or a full Ethiopian meal, if you happen to have one on tap.

• •

120 g (1 cup) white whole wheat flour

150 g (1¼ cups) teff flour

45 g (¼ cup plus 2 tablespoons) millet flour

15 g (2 tablespoons) corn flour (see page 10)

2 teaspoons baking powder

¾ teaspoon fine sea salt

2 cups (470 ml) seltzer water

60 g (¼ cup) unsweetened plain vegan yogurt

Nonstick cooking spray

Whisk together the flours, baking powder, and salt in a medium-size bowl.

Whisk together the seltzer water and yogurt in a small bowl. Pour into the flour mixture and whisk until smooth.

Heat a large nonstick skillet over medium heat. Coat the skillet with cooking spray and do so before every injera. Pour ½ cup (125 g) batter into the skillet and swirl to spread the batter into an 8- to 9-inch (20 to 23 cm) round. Cook for about 4 minutes, until the color darkens and the surface is no longer wet. Remove from the skillet with a spatula and place on a wire rack. When slightly cooled, the injera may be rolled into tubes. Repeat with the remaining batter.

Yield: 6 injera

Spelt and Barley Lemon Cookie Bites

These little glazed cookies boast lots of citrus flavor, making them the perfect sidecar to a cup of tea. Buttery-tasting from the barley flour and lightly sweetened, these are a light and lovely afternoon pick-me-up. Each cookie has only ½ teaspoon oil. But why eat just one?

● ●

¼ cup plus 2 to 3 teaspoons (70 to 75 ml) fresh lemon juice, divided

24 g (2 tablespoons) Sucanat

2 tablespoons (30 ml) neutral-flavored oil

1 tablespoon (15 ml) vegan milk, more if needed

2 teaspoons lemon zest

1 teaspoon pure vanilla extract

140 g (1 cup) whole spelt flour

30 g (¼ cup) barley flour

½ teaspoon baking powder

¼ teaspoon salt

96 g (½ cup) organic turbinado sugar or organic evaporated cane juice

1½ teaspoons cornstarch

Preheat the oven to 350°F (180°C, or gas mark 4). Line a baking sheet with parchment paper or a silicone baking mat.

Combine ¼ cup (60 ml) of the lemon juice, Sucanat, oil, milk, zest, and vanilla in a medium-size bowl. Let stand for 10 minutes, whisking occasionally to dissolve the Sucanat.

Whisk together the flours, baking powder, and salt. Pour the wet ingredients into the dry ingredients and stir together. Add more milk, ½ teaspoon at a time, if needed, to make a soft, shapeable dough.

Using a generous 1 tablespoon (32 g) dough, form into balls and place on the baking sheet 1 inch (2.5 cm) apart. Slightly flatten with your hand. Bake for 9 to 11 minutes, until very lightly browned on the bottom. Transfer the cookies to a wire rack to cool.

While the cookies are cooling, combine the turbinado sugar and cornstarch in a blender. Process until very powdered. Let sit with the lid on for 10 minutes to reduce the dust. Transfer to a small bowl and whisk in 2 teaspoons (10 ml) lemon juice. Whisk until smooth, adding the remaining 1 teaspoon (5 ml) as needed to make a spreadable consistency. When the cookies are cool, coat each cookie with 1 teaspoon of glaze. Continue with any remaining glaze, adding layers to the cookies.

Yield: 12 cookies

Whole and Oats Cookies

We haven't come across anyone who hasn't fallen head over heels for these sturdy cookies in which the add-ins can be switched around (or even dropped) depending on preference, mood, and availability. They are fairly large, too, and make for a perfectly filling snack.

• •

256 g (1 cup) any natural nut butter or seed butter, such as smooth or crunchy natural peanut butter

¼ cup (60 ml) neutral-flavored oil

120 g (½ cup plus 2 tablespoons) organic turbinado sugar or organic evaporated cane juice

120 g (½ cup plus 2 tablespoons) Sucanat

6 tablespoons (90 ml) vegan milk, more if needed

2 teaspoons pure vanilla extract

240 g (2 cups) whole wheat pastry flour

160 g (2 cups) old-fashioned oats or quick-cooking oats

1 teaspoon baking powder

½ teaspoon fine sea salt

50 g (½ cup) chopped pecans (optional, see Note)

80 g (½ cup) raisins or dried cherries (optional, see Note)

Preheat the oven to 375°F (190°C, or gas mark 5). Line 2 baking sheets with parchment paper or silicone baking mats.

In the bowl of a stand mixer fitted with a paddle attachment, combine the nut butter, oil, sugars, milk, and vanilla.

In a large bowl, combine the flour, oats, baking powder, salt, pecans, and cherries.

Add the dry ingredients to the wet and mix to combine. Add extra milk, 1 tablespoon (15 ml) at a time, if the cookie dough is too dry and crumbly. It needs to be moist enough to hold together easily when pinched, without being too wet.

Pack a ¼-cup measure with dough (approximately 90 g per cookie, weight will vary with add-ins), place the dough on the sheet, and flatten slightly, because the cookies won't spread much while baking. Repeat with the remaining dough, placing 7 cookies on each sheet.

Bake for 14 minutes, or until the cookies are golden brown around the edges. Leave the cookies on the baking sheet for 5 minutes before transferring to a wire rack to cool. Let cool completely before storing in an airtight container, at room temperature or in the refrigerator.

Yield: 14 large cookies

Serving Suggestions & Variations

• Pack these with any add-ins you prefer, be it other dried fruits or vegan chocolate chips instead of (or along with) nuts. Just have fun with this recipe and make it your own by switching the ingredients to your liking. These cookies are also great without add-ins, in which case you will get 12 cookies in all.

Kelly's Oatmeal Spelt Cookies

These cookies have crispy edges and a tender, chewy heart. They're like a baked version of the bowl of oatmeal our dear friend Kelly Cavalier, who requested we develop this recipe, loves to eat daily. How's that for a great breakfast on the run? Note that semisolid coconut oil is of the same consistency as slightly softened vegan butter.

• •

13 g (2 tablespoons) flax meal

¼ cup plus 1 to 2 tablespoons (75 to 90 ml) apple cider, divided

96 g (½ cup) Sucanat

¼ cup (60 ml) pure maple syrup

1½ teaspoons ground cinnamon

½ teaspoon fine sea salt

56 g (¼ cup) semisolid coconut oil

1 teaspoon pure vanilla extract

53 g (⅓ cup) chopped dried apple (choose soft dried apples, not too dry)

25 g (¼ cup) pecan halves

80 g (1 cup) quick-cooking oats

140 g (1 cup) whole spelt flour

½ teaspoon baking powder

Preheat the oven to 350°F (180°C, or gas mark 4). Line 2 baking sheets with parchment paper or silicone baking mats.

Combine the flax meal with ¼ cup (60 ml) of the apple cider in a large bowl. Let stand for 5 minutes.

Combine the flax mixture, Sucanat, syrup, cinnamon, salt, oil, and vanilla in the bowl of a stand mixer fitted with the paddle attachment. Mix to combine. In a medium-size bowl, combine the dried apple, pecan halves, oats, flour, and baking powder. Pour the dry ingredients on top of the wet, and mix to combine while adding the remaining 1 to 2 tablespoons (15 to 30 ml) apple cider to obtain a dough that holds together well when pinched and isn't too dry or crumbly.

Pack ¼ cup (75 g) of dough per cookie. Place the dough on the prepared sheets and flatten each cookie almost as much as you will want them to come out of the oven. The cookies won't spread much but they are rather large, so we find it best to bake them 4 per sheet rather than place all 8 on a single sheet.

Bake for 18 minutes, or until they are golden brown and firm on top. Let cool on the sheets for at least 10 minutes before transferring to a wire rack to cool. These are at their best eaten cold from the refrigerator. Store the leftovers in an airtight container in the refrigerator for up to 4 days.

Yield: 8 large cookies

Apple Butter Drops

Inspired by a cookie that Tami's mom used to make, these soft and sweet, bakery-style cookies turned out great with whole grains. With their higher nutritional profile, they're even better than the original. (Sorry, Mom.)

• •

360 g (3 cups) whole wheat pastry flour

60 g (¼ cup plus 2 tablespoons) coconut sugar

1½ teaspoons baking soda

1½ teaspoons ground cinnamon

½ teaspoon fine sea salt

⅓ cup plus 1 tablespoon (90 ml) apple juice, more if needed

⅓ cup plus 1 tablespoon (90 ml) neutral-flavored oil

⅓ cup plus 1 tablespoon (90 ml) pure maple syrup

1½ teaspoons pure vanilla extract

64 g (¼ cup) apple butter

Preheat the oven to 350°F (180°C, or gas mark 4). Line 2 baking sheets with parchment paper or silicone baking mats.

Whisk together the flour, sugar, baking soda, cinnamon, and salt in a medium-size bowl.

Whisk together the apple juice, oil, maple syrup, and vanilla in a small bowl. Pour the wet ingredients into the dry ingredients and stir together. It should be a slightly wet dough, so add an extra 1 or 2 tablespoons (15 to 30 ml) juice, if needed.

Drop 2 tablespoons (44 g) dough onto the baking sheet for each cookie, leaving at least 2 inches (5 cm) between cookies. Make a small indentation with your finger or the back of the spoon in the top of each cookie. Drop 1 teaspoon apple butter into each indentation. Drop another 1 tablespoon (22 g) dough on top of the cookie, partially covering the apple butter, but leaving a bit exposed. Bake the cookies for 15 minutes, until the bottoms have darkened slightly. Let cool on the baking sheet for 5 minutes, then transfer to a wire rack to cool.

Yield: 12 cookies

Serving Suggestions & Variations

• Apple butter lovers might want to add an extra ½ to 1 teaspoon apple butter to each cookie. Be careful, though: If too much is added, the excess will leak out of the cookie onto the baking sheet.

• In a hurry? Fill the indentation as suggested, but omit the top tablespoon of dough to make 18 Apple Butter Thumbprints.

• To make Apple Ginger Drops, add ½ teaspoon ground ginger to the dry ingredients.

Hazelnut Shortbread Fingers

Fact: We've come to love whole wheat pastry flour so much, we now buy it in 25-pound (11 kg) bags. (Also fact: Our kitchen cupboards, refrigerator, and freezer are officially out of storage room.) This versatile flour is brilliant in the following modestly sweetened, richly flavored short-bread fingers that taste great on their own as well as served in the company of any homemade all-fruit jam, or even better, Raspberry Curd (page 46) or Lemon Curd (page 167).

• •

60 g (½ cup) shelled hazelnuts (not skinned)

180 g (1½ cups) whole wheat pastry flour

¼ teaspoon fine sea salt

¼ cup (60 ml) pure maple syrup

¼ cup (60 ml) melted coconut oil

Preheat the oven to 325°F (170°C, or gas mark 3). Line a baking sheet with parchment paper or a silicone baking mat.

Combine the hazelnuts, flour, and salt in a food processor. Process until the hazelnuts are finely ground. Add the maple syrup and oil, pulsing to combine. The dough should be kneadable and not crumbly.

Place the dough on the prepared sheet, knead it for a couple of beats just to make sure it is cohesive, and press it down with your hands or roll it out to form an 8 x 4-inch (20 x 10 cm) rectangle. For thicker fingers, roll out to form an 8 x 3-inch (20 x 8 cm) rectangle.

Cut the rectangle into eight 1-inch (2.5 cm) wide by 4-inch (10 cm) long fingers. Use the tines of a fork to prick the tops of the shortbread. Arrange the fingers on the sheet so that they're about 1 inch (2.5 cm) apart.

Bake for 18 to 22 minutes, or until the fingers are light golden brown around the edges and at the bottom. Carefully transfer to a wire rack to cool.

Store in an airtight container at room temperature for up to 2 days.

Yield: 8 fingers

Serving Suggestions & Variations

- If hazelnuts aren't available, or if you're simply not a big fan of them, use the same quantity of cashews or almonds instead.
- If you'd rather have smaller shortbread fingers, cut the dough into as many shorter, narrower fingers as you wish, but remember to adjust the baking time accordingly.

Kicked-Up Chocolate Cookies

Sweet and spicy is an unbeatable combo, especially when you're talking chocolate. These adult cookies can be made to taste. The cayenne can be omitted for kid-friendly cookies, while the ½ teaspoon is just right for those who can't get enough heat. The ganache and cacao nibs add elegance to these otherwise humble cookies.

• •

68 g (¾ cup) oat flour

79 g (½ cup plus 1 tablespoon) whole spelt flour

15 g (2 tablespoons) barley flour

15 g (3 tablespoons) unsweetened cocoa powder

½ teaspoon baking powder

¼ teaspoon baking soda

¼ teaspoon fine sea salt

¼ to ½ teaspoon cayenne pepper, to taste

⅓ cup (80 ml) vegan milk, more if needed

24 g (2 tablespoons) Sucanat

2 tablespoons (30 ml) neutral-flavored oil

1 tablespoon (15 ml) pure maple syrup

150 g (½ cup) Chocolate Ganache (page 142)

2 teaspoons cacao nibs

Preheat the oven to 350°F (180°C, or gas mark 4). Line a baking sheet with parchment paper or a silicone baking mat.

Whisk together the flours, cocoa, baking powder, baking soda, salt, and cayenne in a medium-size bowl.

Whisk together the milk, Sucanat, oil, and maple syrup in a small bowl. Pour the wet ingredients into the dry ingredients and mix well. The mixture should hold together when packed, with no flour visible. Add an extra 1 tablespoon (15 ml) milk, if needed. Dump the mixture onto a 12-inch (30 cm) piece of parchment paper. Shape into a 4-inch (10 cm) tube.

Cut the dough into eight ½-inch (1.3 cm) slices, patting any crumbly bits back into the cookie and reshaping the cookies into rounds, if needed. Transfer to the baking sheet and bake for 13 to 15 minutes, until the cookies are firmly set and the bottom has slightly darkened. Do not overbake. Let cool on a wire rack.

Spread each cookie with approximately 1 tablespoon (19 g) ganache and sprinkle evenly with the cacao nibs.

Yield: 8 cookies

Ginger and Spice Cookies

Perfectly gingery, with a slight molasses flavor, these cookies will permeate your whole home with a holiday scent that just can't be beat. Gluten-free brown rice flour benefits from the addition of whole spelt flour here to give the cookies a great structure, as well as texture. Note that it's important for all the ingredients used here to be at room temperature and not cold, so that the coconut oil does not further solidify as you mix the dough. (Quick reminder: Semisolid coconut oil is of the same consistency as slightly softened vegan butter.)

• •

44 g (2 tablespoons) molasses

96 g (½ cup) Sucanat

56 g (¼ cup) semisolid coconut oil

8 g (1 tablespoon) cornstarch

2 teaspoons ground ginger

½ teaspoon Chinese five-spice powder
   or pain d'épices spice mix

¼ teaspoon fine sea salt

88 g (½ cup plus 2 tablespoons) whole
   spelt flour

100 g (½ cup plus 2 tablespoons) brown
   rice flour

½ teaspoon baking soda

2 tablespoons (30 ml) vegan milk,
   more if needed

30 g (2 tablespoons) chopped soft
   candied ginger

Preheat the oven to 350°F (180°C, or gas mark 4). Line 2 baking sheets with parchment paper or silicone baking mats.

Combine the molasses, Sucanat, oil, cornstarch, ground ginger, spice powder, and salt in the bowl of a stand mixer fitted with the paddle attachment until well mixed.

In a medium-size bowl, combine the flours and baking soda. Pour the dry ingredients onto the wet, and mix to combine. The mixture will look dry and crumbly. Add the milk, 1 tablespoon (15 ml) at a time, until the dough holds together well when pinched. Add more milk if needed. Mix the chopped ginger into the dough until just combined.

Scoop out 1 tablespoon (24 g) packed dough per cookie, placing 9 of them on each baking sheet. Remove them from the tablespoon and place them flat side (the side that you flattened to pack the dough into the tablespoon) onto the sheet.

Bake for 12 minutes (for slightly chewy cookies) to 15 minutes (for crisper cookies). Leave on the baking sheet for a couple of minutes before placing on a wire rack to cool. Store in an airtight container at room temperature for up to 4 days.

Yield: 18 cookies

Peanut Butter Surprise Cookies

This peanut butter cookie dough is doused with Sriracha sauce for a spicy undercurrent. We've loaded them with chocolate chips, which just burst forth in the flavor thanks to the touch of malty amaranth flour. This unique taste combo might sound a little crazy, but we're willing to bet they will have you coming back for more.

- 85 g (⅓ cup) smooth or crunchy natural peanut butter
- 48 g (¼ cup) organic turbinado sugar or organic evaporated cane juice
- 2 tablespoons (30 ml) neutral-flavored oil
- 1 tablespoon (15 ml) pure maple syrup
- 1 teaspoon pure vanilla extract
- 2 teaspoons Sriracha sauce (see Note)
- 88 g (½ cup) vegan semisweet chocolate chips
- 60 g (½ cup) whole wheat pastry flour
- 23 g (¼ cup) oat flour
- 8 g (1 tablespoon) amaranth flour
- 1 teaspoon baking powder
- ½ teaspoon baking soda
- ½ teaspoon fine sea salt
- ¼ teaspoon Chinese five-spice powder (see Note)
- 2 to 3 tablespoons (30 to 45 ml) vegan milk

Preheat the oven to 350°F (180°C, or gas mark 4). Line a baking sheet with parchment paper or a silicone baking mat.

Combine the peanut butter, sugar, oil, maple syrup, vanilla, and Sriracha in a medium-size bowl. Vigorously stir together with a wooden spoon.

Combine the chocolate chips, flours, baking powder, baking soda, salt, and spice powder in a medium-size bowl. Whisk to combine. Stir into the peanut butter mixture, adding the milk, 1 tablespoon (15 ml) at a time, to make a soft but cohesive dough.

Scoop the dough into a packed, mounded tablespoon (35 g) and drop onto the baking sheet. Slightly press down.

Bake the cookies for 15 to 17 minutes, or until the bottoms are browned. Let cool on the baking sheet on a wire rack for 15 minutes. The cookies will break if moved too soon. Transfer the cookies to the wire rack and let cool completely.

Yield: 12 cookies

Serving Suggestions & Variations

- The Sriracha sauce may be omitted for a less spicy cookie.
- If you don't have (or don't like) Chinese five-spice powder, add ¼ teaspoon ground cinnamon and a pinch of ground white pepper instead.

Whole Wheat Cappuccino Biscotti

Who needs coffee shops to sell us an overpriced cuppa and its faithful compadre, the biscotto, anyway? Make your own cheaper and better version at home instead. Once again, no one will be able to detect the presence of whole grain flour in these biscotti, thanks to the mild flavor of the finely milled whole wheat pastry flour. The only downside to baking these yourself versus buying them ready-made is having to do the dishes once you're done baking. Our advice to you: Eat a couple of biscotti for energy before grabbing that sponge and dish soap. (Tipping not required.)

• •

300 g (2½ cups) whole wheat pastry flour

105 g (¾ cup) dry-roasted or raw cashews

144 g (¾ cup) organic turbinado sugar or organic evaporated cane juice

2½ teaspoons instant espresso granules

½ teaspoon fine sea salt

1½ teaspoons ground cinnamon

1 teaspoon baking powder

¼ cup (60 ml) melted coconut oil or neutral-flavored oil

180 g (¾ cup) vanilla-flavored vegan yogurt

1½ teaspoons pure vanilla extract

1½ teaspoons pure orange extract

88 g (½ cup) vegan semisweet chocolate chips, coarsely chopped

Preheat the oven to 350°F (180°C, or gas mark 4). Line a baking sheet with parchment paper or a silicone baking mat.

Combine the flour, cashews, turbinado sugar, and espresso granules in a food processor. Process until the cashews are finely ground.

Add the salt, cinnamon, and baking powder, pulsing a few times just to combine.

Add the oil, yogurt, and extracts, and pulse to combine until a dough forms. Add the chocolate and pulse a couple of times, just to evenly distribute throughout the dough.

Pat the dough down into a rectangle of 10 x 5 inches (25 x 13 cm). Bake for 30 minutes, until the dough is golden brown around the edges and on top and firm in the center. Remove from the oven and lower the temperature to 325°F (170°C, or gas mark 3).

Let cool on a wire rack. Once cool, use a serrated knife to cut widthwise into approximately ½-inch (1.3 cm) thick slices.

Place the cut slices on their side on the same prepared baking sheet, and bake for 10 minutes, then flip the slices and bake for 10 minutes longer, until both sides are light golden brown, or a bit longer for crispier biscotti.

Let cool on a wire rack. Store in an airtight container at room temperature.

Yield: About 15 biscotti

Jam Crumble Bars

When you bite into the crispy, wholesome crust that partners up so beautifully with a peppy, naturally sweet coulis or jam, you might find yourself having to resist reaching for a second bar right after the first one has been gobbled up.

• •

Nonstick cooking spray

40 g (¼ cup) brown rice flour

140 g (1 cup) whole spelt flour

96 g (½ cup) Sucanat

¼ teaspoon fine sea salt

1 teaspoon ground cinnamon

5 tablespoons (75 ml) melted coconut oil (see Note)

¼ cup (60 ml) vegan milk, as needed

210 g (¾ cup) Berry Coulis made with instant tapioca (recipe variation page 38) or 160 g (½ cup) all-fruit any berry jam

Preheat the oven to 350°F (180°C, or gas mark 4). Coat an 8-inch (20 cm) square pan with cooking spray.

Combine the flours, Sucanat, salt, and cinnamon in a large bowl. Slowly add the oil, stirring to combine. The dough should not look oily (see note). Add the milk, 1 tablespoon (15 ml) at a time, until the dough is just moist enough to stick together when pinched.

Press down two-thirds of the mixture into the prepared pan. Spread the coulis onto the crust, being careful to leave a generous ⅓ inch (8 mm) around the edges. Crumble the remaining one-third of the mixture on top of the coulis.

Bake for 25 minutes, until deep golden brown. Let cool in the pan on a wire rack, then cut into eight 2 x 4-inch (5 x 10 cm) bars. Store in an airtight container in the refrigerator for up to 1 week. These are especially awesome when enjoyed cold from the refrigerator, not to mention easier to cut.

Yield: 8 bars

Recipe Note

It's not too surprising that spelt flour has different levels of absorbency depending on how finely it was milled, that's why we suggest adding the oil slowly, refraining from using the full amount if the dough starts looking oily. If the damage is already done, add more whole spelt flour, 1 tablespoon (9 g) at a time, until the dough is drier, but not too crumbly. If it gets too crumbly, add a little milk to fix it. The dough should easily stick together when pinched.

Caramel Nut Barley Squares

Be the star of your very own vegan bake sale and watch these nutty squares sell like hotcakes. For an added salty boost, sprinkle a few tiny crystals of pink Himalayan salt on top of the chocolate before it firms up. You'll see that it's impossible to tell that a whole grain flour was used to make the shortbreadlike crust. The nuts listed here are merely an example; use any coarsely chopped nuts that you love the most. You should aim for a generous 1¼ cups (weight will vary) of one, or a mix, of your favorite nuts.

. . . .

FOR CRUST:

210 g (1¾ cups) barley flour

¼ teaspoon fine sea salt

¼ cup (60 ml) pure maple syrup or (84 g) raw agave nectar

¼ cup (60 ml) melted coconut oil or neutral-flavored oil

FOR FILLING:

2 tablespoons (30 ml) vegan milk

96 g (½ cup) Sucanat or (80 g) coconut sugar

84 g (¼ cup) brown rice syrup

60 g (½ cup) dry roasted almonds, coarsely chopped

70 g (½ cup) raw cashews or (60 g) hazelnuts, coarsely chopped

30 g (¼ cup) salted pepitas (hulled pumpkin seeds)

1 teaspoon pure vanilla extract

Generous pinch of fine sea salt

88 g (½ cup) vegan semisweet chocolate chips, more if desired

TO MAKE THE CRUST: Preheat the oven to 350°F (180°C, or gas mark 4). For an easier time lifting the bars out of the pan, line an 8-inch (20 cm) square pan with parchment paper, leaving a 2-inch (5 cm) overhang.

Place the flour, salt, and maple syrup in a food processor. Add the oil, 1 tablespoon (15 ml) at a time, until moistened and the dough holds together when pinched. Press down evenly into the prepared pan, with moistened hands if needed. Prebake for 10 minutes, transfer to a wire rack, and leave the oven on. In the meantime, make the filling.

TO MAKE THE FILLING: Place the milk, Sucanat or coconut sugar, and brown rice syrup in a small saucepan over high heat. Bring to a rolling boil, remove from the heat, and add the nuts, vanilla, and the salt, stirring to combine. Sprinkle the nut mixture on top of the crust and use an offset spatula to evenly spread them all over the crust. Bake for 15 minutes longer, or until the caramel is thick and mostly set. Keep a close eye on the nuts so they don't burn.

Remove the pan from the oven, turn the oven off, and place the pan on a wire rack to cool for 5 minutes. Sprinkle the chocolate chips evenly on top. Use more than the amount listed if desired for a thicker chocolate coating. Place the pan back into the oven, and let the residual heat melt the chips for a minute or two. Use an offset spatula to spread the melted chips over the nuts.

Chill in the refrigerator for 1 hour, or until the chocolate is set, before cutting into 2-inch (5 cm) squares. The squares will keep well in an airtight container at room temperature for up to 4 days.

Yield: 16 squares

Take-a-Hike Granola Bars

We've put the usually ubiquitous rolled oats on vacation here by using manganese- and fiber-rich spelt and rye flakes in their place. These perfect hiking companions were described by our testers as being similar to a popular raw chocolate energy bar, but chunkier, much more flavorful, and satisfying, as well as firm yet chewy, but not crunchy or hard. So put a couple of them in your backpack and go explore the world.

● ●

120 g (¾ cup) chopped dates

96 g (1 cup) rolled spelt flakes

96 g (1 cup) rolled rye flakes

40 g (⅓ cup) dry-roasted unsalted almonds, coarsely chopped

60 g (½ cup) dried cranberries

48 g (¼ cup) Sucanat

20 g (¼ cup) unsweetened cocoa powder

1 teaspoon ground cinnamon

60 g (½ cup) salted pepitas (hulled pumpkin seeds)

60 g (¾ cup) unsweetened shredded coconut

¼ teaspoon fine sea salt

¼ cup (60 ml) pure maple syrup

¼ cup (60 ml) neutral-flavored oil

128 g (½ cup) smooth natural peanut butter

1 teaspoon pure vanilla extract

Vegan milk, if needed

Place the dates in a bowl and cover completely with hot water; let soak for 15 minutes, or until the dates are softened. Drain thoroughly and set aside.

Preheat the oven to 350°F (180°C, or gas mark 4). Line a 9 x 13-inch (23 x 33 cm) baking pan with parchment paper. You can either use a stand mixer fitted with a paddle attachment or do it by hand.

Combine the flakes, almonds, cranberries, Sucanat, cocoa powder, cinnamon, pepitas, coconut, and salt in a large bowl.

Place the dates, maple syrup, oil, peanut butter, and vanilla in a food processor. Process until perfectly smooth.

Pour the wet ingredients onto the dry, and stir until thoroughly combined. The preparation will look just a little bit dry but it should stick together when pinched; if it is too dry, add 1 tablespoon (15 ml) or more of vegan milk until it is more cohesive.

Transfer to the prepared pan and press down hard and evenly with moistened hands. Bake for 20 to 25 minutes, or until deep golden brown on top and around the edges. Carefully transfer to a wire rack and let cool completely before cutting. Store in an airtight container in the refrigerator for up to 1 week.

Yield: 16 bars

Chapter 6

Perfectly Wholesome Desserts

Open your piehole and let it do the munching!

From luscious cakes and titillating treats to pies that make the most of the freshest seasonal fruit, these healthier sweets just can't be beat.

Strawberry Sweet Biscuits

We think of these as a sister to the shortcake: Packed with whole grains and rich from the coconut milk and oil, they're an incredibly satisfying dessert. The Sucanat leaves lovely specks of brown, which is where this dessert gets its name. To make it even more decadent, feel free to add a scoop of vegan vanilla ice cream or a dollop of whichever vegan whipped topping you prefer.

⅓ to ⅔ cup (80 to 160 ml) refrigerated coconut milk, divided

1 teaspoon pure vanilla extract

120 g (1 cup) whole wheat pastry flour, plus more for kneading

45 g (½ cup) oat flour

70 g (½ cup) whole spelt flour

12 g (1 tablespoon) baking powder

½ teaspoon fine sea salt

72 g (⅓ cup plus 1 tablespoon) Sucanat, divided

74 g (⅓ cup) semisolid coconut oil

1 quart (714 g) fresh strawberries, hulled and sliced

Preheat the oven to 400°F (200°C, or gas mark 6). Line a baking sheet with parchment paper or a silicone baking mat.

Stir together ⅓ cup (80 ml) of the milk and vanilla in a small bowl.

Combine the flours, baking powder, salt, and 60 g (⅓ cup) of the Sucanat in a food processor. Process until mixed. Add the coconut oil and pulse until the mixture resembles small peas. Pour in the milk mixture and process until the mixture clears the sides of the bowl, adding the remaining ⅓ cup (80 ml) milk as needed. You will probably have 1 tablespoon (15 ml) or more left over. Set aside.

Transfer the dough to a lightly floured surface. Knead it a few times, then pat or roll it into a ½-inch (1.3 cm) thick rectangle. Cut the dough into cakes using a 2½- to 3-inch (6.3 to 7.5 cm) round cutter or decorative cutter of similar size. Pat the dough scraps into a rectangle and cut again until all the dough is used. Transfer the cakes to the baking sheet and place them 2 inches (5 cm) apart. Brush with the remaining 1 tablespoon (15 ml) milk and sprinkle evenly with the remaining 1 tablespoon (12 g) Sucanat. You will not need all of the milk.

Bake for 16 to 18 minutes, or until the bottoms are slightly darkened. Let cool on the baking sheet on a wire rack for 15 minutes. Serve warm or at room temperature with the strawberries.

Yield: 4 to 6 cakes, depending on the size of the cutter

Recipe Note

If your strawberries are less than perfectly ripe, stir some liquid sweetener of choice into the berries to brighten their flavor. Or for a gourmet touch, try a teaspoon of balsamic vinegar.

Chocolate Smorgasbord Spelt Cupcakes

Luscious chocolate ganache on top of a light and moist chocolate cake dotted with chocolate chips? We probably couldn't have made them any more chocolaty. No one will believe these were made with whole grains. (Insider's tip: The fact that naturally sweet-tasting millet flour is rich in iron is our go-to excuse to eat more than one.)

• •

FOR CUPCAKES:

120 g (½ cup) plain or vanilla-flavored vegan yogurt

1 tablespoon (15 ml) apple cider vinegar

2 teaspoons pure vanilla extract

1 cup (235 ml) plain vegan creamer, preferably Silk or MimicCreme brand

144 g (¾ cup) Sucanat

40 g (½ cup) unsweetened cocoa powder

60 g (½ cup) millet flour

105 g (¾ cup) whole spelt flour

¼ teaspoon fine sea salt

1 teaspoon baking soda

66 g (6 tablespoons) vegan semisweet chocolate chips

FOR CHOCOLATE GANACHE:

6 tablespoons (90 ml) plain vegan creamer, preferably Silk or MimicCreme brand

1 teaspoon instant espresso granules (optional)

176 g (1 cup) vegan semisweet chocolate chips

TO MAKE THE CUPCAKES: Preheat the oven to 350°F (180°C, or gas mark 4). Line a standard muffin pan with paper liners.

Use an immersion blender and a bowl or a countertop blender to blend the yogurt, vinegar, vanilla, creamer, Sucanat, and cocoa powder until perfectly smooth.

In a large bowl, whisk together the flours, salt, and baking soda. Add the chocolate chips on top. Pour the wet ingredients onto the dry, and stir until just combined, being careful not to overmix.

Divide the batter evenly among the paper liners, filling them to just below the top. Bake for 18 minutes, or until firm on top. Remove from the pan and let cool on a wire rack.

TO MAKE THE GANACHE: Heat the creamer and espresso granules in a small saucepan over medium heat until warm. Remove from the heat. Add the chips and stir until melted and combined. Let stand for a few minutes until thickened enough to generously spread on the cupcakes.

Yield: 12 cupcakes

Recipe Note

For suggestions on how to use ganache leftovers, see the note in Baked Speculoos Doughnuts (page 30).

Lemony Barley Cupcakes

We might be huge fans of chocolate-based desserts, but we also rarely say no to anything lemony. We love to decorate these moist and light cupcakes with pretty toppers (such as little flags made of kraft paper on toothpicks) to make them look just as irresistible as they taste.

● ●

60 g (½ cup) dry-roasted almonds or almond meal

96 g (½ cup) Sucanat

180 g (1½ cups) barley flour

½ teaspoon ground ginger

½ teaspoon fine sea salt

1 teaspoon baking powder

½ teaspoon baking soda

2 teaspoons lemon zest

½ cup (120 ml) fresh lemon juice

¼ cup (60 ml) pure maple syrup

60 g (¼ cup) plain or vanilla-flavored vegan yogurt

3 tablespoons (45 ml) neutral-flavored oil

Up to 400 g (1¼ cups) chilled Lemon Curd (page 167), as needed

Preheat the oven to 350°F (180°C, or gas mark 4). Line 10 cups of a standard muffin pan with paper liners. Fill the remaining 2 cups halfway with water to ensure even baking and to avoid warping the pan.

Place the almonds and Sucanat in a food processor and process until the almonds are finely ground. If you know your food processor never grinds nuts finely enough, use almond meal instead and skip this step.

Combine the ground almonds (or the almond meal, without forgetting to add the Sucanat), flour, ginger, salt, baking powder, and baking soda in a large bowl.

In another bowl, whisk together the lemon zest, lemon juice, syrup, yogurt, and oil. Pour the wet ingredients onto the dry, and stir until well combined. Divide the batter among the liners, filling about two-thirds full.

Bake for 20 to 22 minutes, or until golden brown, firm on top, and a toothpick inserted into the center comes out clean. Let cool completely before applying the curd.

Place 20 to 40 g (1 to 2 tablespoons) lemon curd on top of each cupcake, using an offset spatula. Decorate with pretty cupcake toppers. These cupcakes are best when enjoyed the day they're baked.

Yield: 10 cupcakes

Recipe Note

The almond flavor will be more pronounced when using dry-roasted whole almonds instead of plain almond meal, but if your food processor doesn't grind the almonds finely enough, use almond meal.

Pineapple Upside-Down Cupcakes

Upside-down cupcakes are long overdue, so we bring to you these perfectly sweetened, lightly spiced, pineapple-topped cuppers. With just the right ratio of pineapple to tender cake, they will please the pineapple lovers in your life.

. . . .

FOR PINEAPPLE MIXTURE:

110 g (¼ cup plus 2 tablespoons) drained, crushed pineapple

24 g (2 tablespoons) organic turbinado sugar

8 g (1 tablespoon) cornstarch

FOR CUPCAKES:

Nonstick cooking spray

¼ cup plus 2 tablespoons (90 ml) Muscat wine (see Note)

⅓ cup (80 ml) refrigerated coconut milk

¼ cup (60 ml) neutral-flavored oil

48 g (¼ cup) organic turbinado sugar or organic evaporated cane juice

30 g (2 tablespoons) plain or vanilla-flavored vegan yogurt

7 g (1 tablespoon) flax meal

2 teaspoons pure vanilla extract

150 g (1¼ cups) whole wheat pastry flour

23 g (¼ cup) oat flour

2 teaspoons baking powder

½ teaspoon baking soda

½ teaspoon fine sea salt

½ teaspoon ground cinnamon

Pinch of ground nutmeg

TO MAKE THE PINEAPPLE MIXTURE: Stir all the ingredients together in a small bowl and set aside.

TO MAKE THE CUPCAKES: Preheat the oven to 375°F (190°C, or gas mark 5). Heavily coat 8 cups of a standard muffin pan with cooking spray. Fill the remaining 4 cups halfway with water to ensure even baking and to avoid warping the pan. Divide the pineapple mixture evenly among the cups, using a scant 1 tablespoon for each.

Whisk the wine, milk, oil, sugar, yogurt, flax meal, and vanilla together in a medium-size bowl. In a second medium-size bowl, whisk together the flours, baking powder, baking soda, salt, cinnamon, and nutmeg. Pour the wet ingredients into the dry and stir to combine, but do not overmix.

Scoop 3 tablespoons (36 g) cake batter into each cup. Bake for 18 to 20 minutes, or until the cupcakes are golden and a toothpick inserted into the center comes out clean. Cool the cupcakes in the muffin pan on a wire rack for 30 minutes. Then turn over to release the cakes. If any pineapple adheres to the pan, pat it back onto the cake top.

Yield: 8 cupcakes

Recipe Note

Muscat is a sweet white dessert wine. If it isn't available, Sauternes, Riesling Spätlese, or other sweet white wine may be substituted. The pineapple juice from the crushed pineapple can also be used here for a nonalcoholic version.

Layered Chocolate and Banana Mini Cakes

These mini cakes are perfect for gifting and sharing the whole grain love, and they make a guaranteed bake sale favorite. They are moderately sweet, but the addition of chocolate chips magically turns them into a dessert item. Don't worry if you cannot get the bananas perfectly smooth when you mash them: Tiny bits of banana sprinkled throughout the cakes are actually pretty great.

Nonstick cooking spray

180 g (1½ cups) whole wheat pastry flour

66 g (6 tablespoons) vegan semisweet chocolate chips

2 teaspoons baking powder

½ teaspoon fine sea salt

260 g (1¾ cups) sliced banana (about 3 small), mashed

120 g (½ cup plus 2 tablespoons) Sucanat

⅓ cup (80 ml) neutral-flavored oil

8 g (1 tablespoon) cornstarch

1 teaspoon pure vanilla extract

10 g (2 tablespoons) unsweetened cocoa powder

Preheat the oven to 350°F (180°C, or gas mark 4). Lightly coat two 5¾ x 3-inch (14 x 8 cm) loaf pans with cooking spray.

In a large bowl, combine the flour, chocolate chips, baking powder, and salt. In a medium-size bowl, combine the banana, Sucanat, oil, cornstarch, and vanilla. Pour the wet ingredients into the dry, and stir until just combined.

Place half of the batter in a medium-size bowl. Stir the cocoa powder into one of the bowls.

Divide the non-chocolate batter among the prepared pans. Divide the chocolate batter among the prepared pans, placing it on top of the non-chocolate batter and smoothing the tops with an angled spatula.

Bake for 30 to 35 minutes, checking after 20 minutes to see if the cakes brown up too quickly and loosely covering them with foil if they do. Insert a toothpick into the center of the loaves to check for doneness. The cakes should be firm on top. Carefully remove from the pan and let cool completely before slicing.

Yield: 2 mini loaves

Berry Streusel Cupcakes

These cute little cakes would be suitable for breakfast, because they are not overly sweet. You could use all-fruit, unsweetened jam if you're in a pinch, instead of berry coulis or curd, but the cakes are at their best with homemade fruity deliciousness. The whole wheat pastry flour gives them a great, tender texture while remaining subtle enough in taste to let the other important flavors shine through.

FOR STREUSEL:

8 g (1 tablespoon) whole wheat pastry flour

23 g (3 tablespoons) almond meal

24 g (2 tablespoons) Sucanat

½ teaspoon ground cinnamon

1 tablespoon (15 ml) vegan creamer

FOR CUPCAKES:

2 tablespoons (30 ml) neutral-flavored oil

60 g (5 tablespoons) Sucanat

60 g (¼ cup) plain or vanilla-flavored vegan yogurt

6 tablespoons (90 ml) vegan milk

1 teaspoon pure vanilla extract

150 g (1¼ cups) whole wheat pastry flour

1 teaspoon baking powder

¼ teaspoon fine sea salt

70 g (¼ cup) Berry Coulis (page 38) or Raspberry Curd (page 46)

TO MAKE THE STREUSEL: Combine the flour, almond meal, Sucanat, and cinnamon in a small bowl. Work the creamer (add it 1 teaspoon at a time; you might not need all of it) into the preparation, just until coarse crumbs form. Set aside.

TO MAKE THE CUPCAKES: Preheat the oven to 350°F (180°C, or gas mark 4). Line 8 cups of a standard muffin pan with paper liners. Fill the remaining 4 cups halfway with water to ensure even baking and to avoid warping the pan.

Combine the oil, Sucanat, yogurt, milk, and vanilla in a large bowl. Combine the flour, baking powder, and salt in a medium-size bowl. Pour the dry ingredients onto the wet and stir just until combined.

Divide the batter evenly among the paper liners, filling them about halfway full. Place 1½ teaspoons of the coulis or curd on top of the batter in each liner. Carefully swirl with the tip of a butter knife, holding the paper liner as you do this. Divide the streusel evenly among the cakes, using a generous 1½ teaspoons for each. Place a large piece of parchment paper under the muffin pan, in case of spillage. Bake for 24 minutes, or until the cakes are golden brown and firm on top. Let cool on a wire rack.

Yield: 8 cupcakes

Mini Lime Bundt Cakes

Heads up! These tender, prettily shaped cakes are to be paired with lime curd, so make your life easier by preparing the curd a day ahead to cut down on prep time, and to give the curd enough time to thoroughly chill before diving in, fork first. Barley flour has a lower gluten content than whole wheat flour does, a fact that, along with the flour's slightly sweet flavor, makes it exceptionally well suited for dessert items, and which makes for tender results. We love the (perhaps surprising) addition of mashed avocado here, which imparts a rich, buttery flavor to the cake.

• •

Nonstick cooking spray

180 g (1½ cups) barley flour

2 teaspoons baking powder

¼ teaspoon fine sea salt

115 g (½ cup) mashed avocado

120 g (¾ cup) coconut sugar

¼ cup (60 ml) pure maple syrup

¼ cup (60 ml) melted coconut oil or neutral-flavored oil

¼ cup plus 2 tablespoons (90 ml) lime juice (zest the lime before juicing it!)

8 g (1 tablespoon) cornstarch

2 teaspoons pure vanilla extract

1 teaspoon lime zest

1 recipe Lemon Curd (page 167), made with lime juice instead of lemon juice

Preheat the oven to 350°F (180°C, or gas mark 4). Lightly coat four 4½-inch (11 cm) Bundt pans with cooking spray.

Combine the flour, baking powder, and salt in a large bowl.

To get the smoothest results, blend the avocado, sugar, syrup, oil, lime juice, cornstarch, and vanilla in a blender.

Pour the wet ingredients onto the dry, along with the lime zest, and stir until combined. The color of the batter won't be pretty at this point, but the cakes will be gorgeous once baked.

Divide the batter evenly among the prepared pans. Bake for 27 minutes, or until golden brown and firm and a toothpick inserted into the center comes out clean.

Remove the cakes from the pans, turning the cakes upside down. Let cool completely on a wire rack before placing the cakes on a plate and filling the cake holes with the curd. Serve with extra curd, if desired.

Yield: 4 mini Bundt cakes

Wholesome Vanilla Pound Cake

This moderately sweet dessert, reminiscent of pound cake but not quite as heavy and dense, is the perfect vehicle to build yourself some quick shortcakes, alongside cashew cream and fresh strawberries (or other seasonal berries), or to simply enjoy with jam or curd. Whole wheat pastry flour is the star of the show here: its lower gluten content, compared to regular whole wheat flour, makes it the perfect substitute for all-purpose flour in baked goods that contain no yeast, but the fact that it retains its best nutritional attributes makes it far more valuable to your health. (And palate!)

• •

Nonstick cooking spray

240 g (1 cup) vanilla-flavored vegan yogurt

¾ cup (180 ml) pure maple syrup

¼ cup (60 ml) melted coconut oil

1 tablespoon (15 ml) pure vanilla extract

24 g (3 tablespoons) cornstarch or arrowroot powder

180 g (1½ cups) whole wheat pastry flour

2 teaspoons baking powder

⅛ teaspoon fine sea salt

2 teaspoons lemon zest

Preheat the oven to 350°F (180°C, or gas mark 4). Lightly coat a 7¾ x 3¾-inch (19.5 x 9.5 cm) loaf pan with cooking spray. A regular 8 x 4-inch (20 x 10 cm) loaf pan will do as well, but the loaf will just be slightly flatter.

Combine the yogurt, maple syrup, oil, vanilla, and cornstarch in a blender, or use an immersion blender and a bowl, and blend until perfectly smooth. You need to do this at room temperature because the coconut oil will solidify as it hits cold ingredients.

Transfer to a large bowl. Combine the flour, baking powder, salt, and zest in another bowl. Pour the dry ingredients on top of the wet, and stir until well combined. Pour into the prepared pan.

Bake for 45 minutes, or until firm and a toothpick inserted into the center comes out clean. Check after approximately 30 minutes of baking, and if the cake browns too quickly, loosely cover it with foil. Let cool for 15 minutes on a wire rack before removing the cake from the pan. Let the cake cool completely before slicing. Leftovers can be stored in an airtight container at room temperature for up to 2 days.

Yield: 1 loaf

Nectarine-Topped Oatmeal Cake

We've learned that cashews make a rich cake base, allowing us to use a little less sweetener and oil. Perfect nectarines are like perfect avocados: They don't happen as often as we'd like, but when they do, they're sublime. The next time you happen upon the ultimate nectarines, make this wholesome, tender-crumbed cake.

• •

Nonstick cooking spray

½ cup (120 ml) apple juice,
   more if needed

47 g (⅓ cup) cashews

¼ cup (60 ml) maple syrup

7 g (1 tablespoon) flax meal

80 g (⅓ cup) unsweetened applesauce

¼ cup (60 ml) neutral-flavored oil

1 teaspoon pure vanilla extract

90 g (1 cup plus 2 tablespoons)
   quick-cooking oats, divided

120 g (1 cup) whole wheat pastry flour

45 g (½ cup) oat flour

2 teaspoons baking powder

1 teaspoon baking soda

¾ teaspoon ground cinnamon

½ teaspoon fine sea salt

Pinch of grated nutmeg

2 nectarines, pitted and sliced

24 g (2 tablespoons) Sucanat

Preheat the oven to 350°F (180°C, or gas mark 4). Lightly coat an 8-inch (20 cm) round cake pan with cooking spray.

Combine the apple juice, cashews, maple syrup, and flax meal in a blender. Process until completely smooth. Add the applesauce, oil, and vanilla. Process until blended.

Whisk together 80 g (1 cup) of the oats, the flours, baking powder, baking soda, cinnamon, salt, and nutmeg in a medium-size bowl. Pour the cashew mixture into the oat mixture and stir to combine. The mixture will be thick but spreadable. If necessary, add an extra 1 tablespoon (15 ml) apple juice. Spread the batter in the pan and arrange the nectarine slices on top.

Combine the remaining 10 g (2 tablespoons) oats and Sucanat in a small bowl. Sprinkle over the top of the cake, gently pressing it into the cake with flat hands. Bake for 35 to 40 minutes, or until a toothpick inserted into the center comes out clean. Let cool on a wire rack before slicing.

Yield: One 8-inch (20 cm) cake

Recipe Note

If the nectarines at your market aren't tempting, opt for peaches or apples instead.

Better with Beans Brownies

These brownies are intensely chocolaty but definitely not overly sweet and make use of a now pretty common baked good ingredient: cooked beans. You know by now with the many recipes available online (and in our previous books) that the beans are absolutely not noticeable, but they work their magic in perfect unison with the whole spelt flour here to add even more fiber and structure to what might very well become your new favorite and actually pretty good-for-you brownie.

Nonstick cooking spray

10 ounces (285 g) vegan semisweet chocolate chips, divided

¼ cup (60 ml) neutral-flavored oil

80 g (½ cup) coconut sugar or (96 g) Sucanat

¼ cup (60 ml) pure maple syrup

¼ teaspoon fine sea salt

2 teaspoons pure vanilla extract

1 can (15 ounces, or 425 g) cannellini beans, drained and rinsed

123 g (¾ cup plus 2 tablespoons) whole spelt flour

10 g (2 tablespoons) unsweetened cocoa powder

⅜ teaspoon baking powder

Preheat the oven to 350°F (180°C, or gas mark 4). Lightly coat an 8-inch (20 cm) square pan with cooking spray.

Combine 8 ounces (227 g) of the chocolate chips and the oil in a small microwave-safe bowl. Heat in 1-minute increments, and stir, heating again slowly, until the chocolate melts easily when stirred. Be careful not to scorch the chocolate. Alternatively, melt the chips and oil in a double boiler.

Combine the sugar, syrup, salt, vanilla, and beans in a food processor. Process until completely smooth, stopping occasionally to scrape down the sides with a rubber spatula.

Add the chocolate mixture to the food processor, and process until combined and smooth. Add the flour, cocoa, and baking powder. Process until smooth, stopping occasionally to scrape down the sides with a rubber spatula. Add the remaining 2 ounces (58 g) chocolate chips to the food processor, and pulse a few times just to evenly distribute the chips through-out the batter. Pour the batter into the prepared pan, using an offset spatula to evenly spread it out.

Bake for 20 minutes, until firm on top. Do not overbake the brownies.

Let cool on a wire rack before removing from the pan and cutting into sixteen 2-inch (5 cm) squares. They are amazing eaten still warm, but they will be a bit crumbly at that stage. They are less friable when eaten at room temperature. We do not recommend keeping these in the refrigerator, because it makes them a touch bitter. Enjoy within 2 days of preparation, stored in an airtight container at room temperature.

If you have leftover ganache from another one of our recipes (pages 30 & 142), consider spreading as much as you like on top of these brownies for a decadent touch.

Yield: 16 brownies

Whole Wheat Peanut Blondies

These rich peanutty blondies make for a great tea or coffee accompaniment when you just need to unwind from a frustrating day. Far tastier than punching pillows! Cut them (the blondies, not the pillows) into small squares for maximum enjoyment.

The flour used here, graham flour, is slightly coarser than other whole wheat flours. That's because the components of the wheat berries are ground separately: The endosperm is finely ground, while the bran and germ are coarsely ground. It is usually used for pie crusts or cookies, but we love it in this application. Feel free to use either whole wheat pastry flour, or even white whole wheat flour, in its place.

• •

Nonstick cooking spray

135 g (1 cup plus 2 tablespoons) graham flour, white whole wheat flour, or whole wheat pastry flour, divided

½ cup (120 ml) water

96 g (½ cup) organic turbinado sugar or organic evaporated cane juice

192 g (¾ cup) smooth natural peanut butter

2 teaspoons pure vanilla extract

½ teaspoon fine sea salt

¼ teaspoon baking powder

55 g (⅓ cup) vegan semisweet chocolate chips

Preheat the oven to 350°F (180°C, or gas mark 4). Lightly coat an 8-inch (20 cm) square pan with cooking spray.

Place 30 g (¼ cup) of the flour with the water in a small saucepan, whisking to combine. Bring to a boil, lower the heat, and cook until thickened like paste, about 1 minute, whisking constantly. Remove from the heat and set aside.

Place the sugar and the remaining 105 g (¾ cup plus 2 tablespoons) flour in a food processor. Process for 1 minute. Add the peanut butter, vanilla, salt, and flour paste, processing until combined. The batter, which will almost look like cookie dough, will form a ball at this point. It should be moist. Add the chocolate chips and pulse only a couple of times, just to evenly distribute the chips throughout the batter.

Transfer to the prepared pan and press down evenly. Bake for 20 minutes, until golden brown on the edges and firm on top. Do not overbake.

Place the pan on a wire rack to cool before slicing into sixteen 2-inch (5 cm) squares. These fudgy blondies are best enjoyed straight from the refrigerator, and they are also easier to cut once chilled in the pan.

Yield: 16 blondies

Serving Suggestions & Variations
The peanut butter can be replaced with roasted almond butter or cashew butter.

Mini Pecan Pies

We've maximized the nut flavor and fiber content in these little bites of bliss by using spelt flour alongside the pecans that appear in both the crust and the filling. Note that if your dates are a little dry, you can soak them in hot water for 5 to 10 minutes until they are softer, then drain them well before use.

• •

FOR CRUST:

Nonstick cooking spray

75 g (¾ cup) pecan halves

210 g (1½ cups) whole spelt flour

⅛ teaspoon fine sea salt

3 tablespoons (45 ml) neutral-flavored oil

2 tablespoons (30 ml) pure maple syrup

6 tablespoons (90 ml) cold apple juice concentrate or apple cider, as needed

FOR FILLING:

150 g (½ cup plus 2 tablespoons) firm silken tofu

5 soft pitted dates

48 g (¼ cup) organic turbinado sugar or organic evaporated cane juice

2½ tablespoons (38 ml) pure maple syrup

9 g (1¼ tablespoons) flax meal

1¼ teaspoons pure vanilla extract

1¼ teaspoons instant espresso granules (optional)

Pinch of fine sea salt

94 g (¾ cup plus 3 tablespoons) pecan halves, chopped

TO MAKE THE CRUST: Preheat the oven to 375°F (190°C, or gas mark 5). Lightly coat 32 cups in 2 mini cupcake pans with cooking spray. Fill the remaining 16 cups halfway with water to ensure even baking and to avoid warping the pan.

Combine the pecan halves, flour, and salt in a food processor. Process until the nuts are completely ground. Add the oil and maple syrup, and pulse a few times. Add the apple juice, 1 tablespoon (15 ml) at a time, until the dough holds together well when pinched and is sufficiently moist. Grab about 2 teaspoons of the crust mixture, and press into each cup, using your thumbs, covering the bottom and sides of the cups. Set aside.

TO MAKE THE FILLING: Combine the tofu, dates, sugar, maple syrup, flax meal, vanilla, espresso granules, and salt in a small food processor. Process until smooth. Stir in the pecans. Spoon approximately 2 teaspoons of filling into each crust. Bake for 16 minutes, until the crust is golden and the filling is set. Using a spoon, carefully move the pies from the pan to a wire rack to cool.

Yield: 32 mini pies

Peach Pielets

The slightly crisp, maple-sweetened crust is the ideal vessel for fresh peaches. These adorable deep-dish pies disappear quickly, whether it's as dessert or on a bake sale table. They are sure to be popular at any gathering, so you might want to double the recipe.

• •

Nonstick cooking spray

FOR FILLING:

500 g (2¾ cups) peeled, sliced peaches, cut in half

1½ tablespoons (23 ml) pure maple syrup

24 g (3 tablespoons) whole wheat pastry flour

¼ teaspoon ground cinnamon

Pinch of fine sea salt

FOR CRUST:

180 g (1½ cups) barley flour

105 g (¾ cup) whole spelt flour

90 g (¾ cup) whole wheat pastry flour

½ teaspoon fine sea salt

½ cup plus 1 tablespoon (135 ml) neutral-flavored oil

3 tablespoons (45 ml) pure maple syrup

¼ cup plus 2 tablespoons (90 ml) vegan milk, divided, plus extra for finishing the pielets

1 teaspoon organic turbinado sugar

Preheat the oven to 400°F (200°C, or gas mark 6). Lightly coat 10 of the cups of a standard muffin pan with cooking spray. Fill the remaining 2 cups halfway with water to ensure even baking and to avoid warping the pan.

TO MAKE THE FILLING: Stir all the ingredients together in a medium-size bowl.

TO MAKE THE CRUST: Whisk together the flours and salt in a medium-size bowl. Stir together the oil and maple syrup in a small bowl. Drizzle the oil/syrup mixture into the flours, and stir with a fork. The flour should resemble crumbs. Add ¼ cup (60 ml) of the milk and stir with a fork. Add the remaining 1 to 2 tablespoons (15 to 30 ml) milk if needed, to make a dough that holds together when pinched.

Fill the cups with a scant 3 tablespoons (60 g) of dough. Press the dough onto the sides and bottom of the cups. Spoon a heaping ¼ cup (50 g) filling into each cup.

Pat or roll out the remaining dough on a lightly floured surface to ¼-inch (6 mm) thickness. Using a small cookie cutter, cut 10 shapes. Place the shapes on top of the filling. Lightly brush the shapes with milk and sprinkle with the turbinado sugar.

Bake for 23 to 27 minutes, until the edges are slightly browned. Let the pielets sit in the pan for 10 minutes, then loosen carefully with a butter knife and lift from the pan. You may need to gently tip the pan and guide the pielets from it. Let cool on a wire rack until serving.

Yield: 10 pielets

Recipe Note

The sweetness of fresh fruit varies, so feel free to add more maple syrup to the filling to suit your taste.

Lazy Lattice Cherry Bars

You know the saying "Baseball, not-dogs, apple pie, and lemonade"? Not in Tami's family. Mouth-puckering sour cherry pie is the family favorite. Making pies is a labor of love, but sometimes cutting corners can be a good thing. This quick bar cookie version is lower in fat than a typical double crust pie, but still delivers on taste.

● ●

Nonstick cooking spray

FOR FILLING:

1 can (14½ ounces, or 451 g) pitted red tart cherries, drained

20 g (2 tablespoons) coconut sugar

24 g (2 tablespoons) instant tapioca, such as Let's Do...Organic

12 g (1 tablespoon) Sucanat

¾ teaspoon ground cinnamon

½ teaspoon almond extract

FOR CRUST:

60 g (½ cup) almonds or almond meal

90 g (¾ cup) whole wheat pastry flour

68 g (¾ cup) oat flour

15 g (2 tablespoons) barley flour

21 g (3 tablespoons) finely ground cornmeal

40 g (¼ cup) coconut sugar

12 g (1 tablespoon) Sucanat

7 g (1 tablespoon) flax meal

¼ teaspoon fine sea salt

¼ cup (60 ml) neutral-flavored oil

¼ cup (60 ml) vegan milk, more if needed

Preheat the oven to 375°F (190°C, or gas mark 5). Lightly coat an 8-inch (20 cm) square pan with cooking spray.

TO MAKE THE FILLING: Combine all the ingredients in a medium-size saucepan over medium heat. Cook, stirring, for 5 minutes, until bubbly and thickened to a jam consistency. Set aside while making the crust. The tapioca will still be visible, but will disappear when the bars are cool.

TO MAKE THE CRUST: Put the almonds in a food processor and process until powdered. Add the flours, cornmeal, sugars, flax meal, and salt. Process until well combined. Drizzle in the oil and process the mixture into crumbs. Drizzle in the milk, as needed, to make a cohesive crust that can be pinched together. Process until the crust forms a ball and clears the sides of the food processor bowl.

Remove a generous ½ cup (145 g) of dough. Lightly flour a work surface and roll the dough into a 5 x 9-inch (13 x 23 cm) rectangle. Use a rotary cookie cutter with a scalloped edge to cut the rectangle into 5 strips measuring 1-inch (2.5 cm) wide and 9-inches (23 cm) long. Press the remaining dough thinly and evenly into the prepared pan. Press the dough up the sides of the pan about ½ inch (1.3 cm). Spread the cherry filling evenly over the dough. Top with the strips, laying 3 strips evenly across the dough, then laying the remaining 2 strips perpendicular. Lightly press the ends of the strips onto the rimmed edge of the dough on the bottom layer.

Bake for 20 to 23 minutes, until golden brown. Let cool for 30 minutes before cutting into 12 bars 2 x 2⅔ inches (5 x 6.8 cm).

Yield: 12 bars

Cranapple Crumble Pie

In New England, the fruit of the orchard and the bounty of the cranberry bogs are a classic combination. It's no wonder New Englanders think a slice of pie is the ideal breakfast. In fact, they're on to something. Because some people prefer crust to a crumble, we've used both here to make the perfect pie. Vital wheat gluten makes the crust a little more flexible and easier to handle.

• •

FOR CRUST:

60 g (½ cup) whole wheat pastry flour

30 g (⅓ cup) oat flour

40 g (⅓ cup) barley flour

18 g (2 tablespoons) vital wheat gluten

¼ teaspoon fine sea salt

1 teaspoon pure maple syrup

1 teaspoon apple cider vinegar

¼ cup (60 ml) neutral-flavored oil

3 to 4 tablespoons (45 to 60 ml) cold apple juice

FOR FILLING:

880 g (8 cups) peeled, cored, and thinly sliced baking apples

100 g (1 cup) fresh or frozen cranberries

Juice from ½ lemon

96 g (½ cup) organic turbinado sugar or organic evaporated cane juice

30 g (⅓ cup) oat flour

1 teaspoon ground cinnamon

FOR TOPPING:

60 g (½ cup) whole wheat pastry flour

45 g (½ cup) oat flour

64 g (⅓ cup) organic turbinado sugar or organic evaporated cane juice

20 g (¼ cup) old-fashioned rolled oats

1 teaspoon ground cinnamon

¼ cup (60 ml) neutral-flavored oil

Preheat the oven to 375°F (190°C, or gas mark 5).

TO MAKE THE CRUST: Combine the flours, gluten, and salt in a food processor and process until combined. Add the maple syrup, vinegar, and oil. Pulse to form small crumbs. Drizzle in the apple juice, 1 tablespoon (15 ml) at a time, pulsing, until the dough can be pinched together and holds its shape.

Transfer the dough to a lightly floured piece of parchment paper, and roll into a 12-inch (30 cm) round. Invert a 9-inch (23 cm) pie plate on top of the round and carefully turn over so the crust is in the pie plate. Gently press it into the pan and crimp the edge. Place the crust in the refrigerator while preparing the rest of the pie.

TO MAKE THE FILLING: Combine all the ingredients in a large bowl. Stir gently to coat the fruit. Spread evenly in the pie crust. If any apple ends are poking up, they may burn.

TO MAKE THE TOPPING: Combine the flours, sugar, oats, and cinnamon in a medium-size bowl. Stir together with a fork. Drizzle in the oil and stir until the mixture is crumbly. Sprinkle evenly over the filling.

Place the pie on a baking sheet in case the filling spills over. Bake for 55 to 60 minutes, until the top is golden and the filling is bubbly. Cool slightly before cutting.

Yield: One 9-inch (23 cm) pie

Whole Wheat Almond Plum Crostatas

Wondering how to use the muffin top pan that's been sadly relegated to a faraway cupboard? These crispy and fruity crostatas will actually shape and hold best when baked in such a pan. If you do not have a muffin top pan, you can use individual pie pans of approximately 4 inches (10 cm) in diameter. If the season is right, you can replace the plums with 2 to 4 firm apricots, depending on size.

• •

FOR CRUST:

Nonstick cooking spray

150 g (1¼ cups) whole wheat pastry flour

48 g (¼ cup) organic turbinado sugar or organic evaporated cane juice

Scant ½ teaspoon fine sea salt

¼ cup (60 ml) neutral-flavored oil

Vegan milk, as needed

FOR FILLING:

60 g (½ cup) almond meal

2 teaspoons cornstarch

55 g (¼ cup plus 1 heaping tablespoon) organic turbinado sugar or organic evaporated cane juice, divided

½ teaspoon pure almond extract or 1 teaspoon pure vanilla extract

2 teaspoons vegan milk

2 large, quite firm plums, pitted and cut into thin wedges

TO MAKE THE CRUST: Preheat the oven to 375°F (190°C, or gas mark 5). Lightly coat 4 cups of a muffin top pan or 4 individual 4-inch (10 cm) pans with cooking spray.

Place the flour, sugar, and salt in a food processor. Process until no large sugar crystals remain. Add the oil while pulsing to combine. Add just enough milk for the dough to stick together easily when pinched, 1 tablespoon (15 ml) at a time, as you hit the pulse button.

Form the dough into a ball, and divide it into 4 equal portions. Roll out each portion of dough into a circle measuring a generous 5 inches (13 cm) in diameter.

Transfer the disks of dough to the prepared cups. If the dough tears a little during the transfer, simply patch the holes with your fingers.

TO MAKE THE FILLING: Place the almond meal, cornstarch, and 48 g (¼ cup) of the sugar in a food processor. Process until no large sugar crystals remain. Add the almond extract and milk while pulsing to combine. Divide the filling among the 4 crusts, 1 heaping tablespoon (28 g) filling per crostata. Crumble it evenly on the bottom of each crust and press down a little. Divide the plum wedges among the 4 crusts, one pointy end of a wedge centered in the middle of the crust, and each wedge slightly overlapping the previous one. Carefully fold the crust overhang over the filling. Sprinkle each top with a scant teaspoon sugar.

Line the oven rack with aluminum foil or a baking sheet just in case the juice from the fruit should escape. Bake for 30 minutes, or until the crust is golden brown and the plums are tender. Carefully remove from the pan and transfer to a wire rack to cool, because the crostatas are at their best when fully cooled. They will also remain fresh and crisp when tightly wrapped and stored in the refrigerator for up to 2 days.

Yield: 4 crostatas

Mango Blackberry Crumble

Make this dessert in spring when mangoes are at their best, or rely on frozen fruit to enjoy it year-round. Frozen fruit has an advantage: It tends to be more predictably ripe. However, if mangoes are in season, lucky you! Just sweeten them to taste. You'll probably need 2 or 3, depending on size. The lightly sweetened crumble topping has the perfect texture to bring out the best in the fruit, whether fresh or frozen.

• •

1 pound (4 cups, or 454 g) fresh or frozen mango chunks, thawed

379 g (2 cups) fresh or frozen blackberries, thawed

5 tablespoons (75 ml) pure maple syrup, divided, more if needed

16 g (2 tablespoons) cornstarch

1½ teaspoons minced fresh rosemary or ½ teaspoon dried (optional)

1 teaspoon pure vanilla extract

90 g (1 cup) oat flour

105 g (¾ cup) whole spelt flour

23 g (3 tablespoons) barley flour

7 g (1 tablespoon) flax meal

¾ teaspoon ground cinnamon

Pinch of fine sea salt

⅓ cup (80 ml) neutral-flavored oil

Preheat the oven to 400°F (200°C, or gas mark 6).

Stir together the mangoes, blackberries, 2 tablespoons (30 ml) of the maple syrup, cornstarch, rosemary, and vanilla in a large bowl. Taste and add an extra 1 tablespoon (15 ml) maple syrup if you prefer sweeter fruit. Pour the fruit into an 8-inch (20 cm) square baking dish. Place on a baking sheet in case the filling spills over during baking.

Combine the flours, flax meal, cinnamon, and salt in a medium-size bowl. Stir together with a fork. Drizzle in the oil and the remaining 3 tablespoons (45 ml) maple syrup. Stir together to form a crumble. Use your fingers to break the crumble into bits and sprinkle it evenly over the fruit.

Bake for 25 to 30 minutes, until the fruit bubbles and the crisp is slightly golden. Serve hot, warm, or at room temperature.

Yield: One 8-inch (20 cm) crumble

Recipe Notes

• This recipe is very versatile. Feel free to adapt the fruit to whatever you prefer.

• If your fruit is a bit tart, add an extra 1 tablespoon (15 ml) maple syrup to sweeten it to taste.

Stone-Fruit Cobbler

Warm from the oven, this cobbler shows why the kitchen is the heart of the home. Our very favorite version of this is made from a combo of fruit, such as peaches and plums, but it's also wonderful made with just one variety. Even healthier, there is no oil in this recipe.

• •

990 g (6 cups) peeled, pitted, and sliced fruit of choice (plums, peaches, mangoes, or other stone fruit)

24 g (3 tablespoons) cornstarch, more if needed

60 g (5 tablespoons) organic turbinado sugar or organic evaporated cane juice, divided, more if needed

1 tablespoon (15 ml) fresh lemon juice

¾ teaspoon ground cinnamon

Pinch of ground nutmeg

90 g (1 cup) oat flour

60 g (½ cup) barley flour

2 teaspoons baking powder

¼ teaspoon fine sea salt

¼ cup (60 ml) vegan milk

60 g (¼ cup) vanilla-flavored vegan yogurt

Preheat the oven to 350°F (180°C, or gas mark 4). Place four 12-ounce (341 g) oven-safe ramekins on a baking sheet, or if preferred, bake in a 9-inch (23 cm) baking pan.

Combine the fruit, cornstarch, 36 g (3 tablespoons) of the sugar, lemon juice, cinnamon, and nutmeg in a medium-size saucepan. Cook over medium heat, stirring occasionally, for 5 minutes, or until thickened. Divide the mixture evenly among the ramekins.

In a medium-size bowl, whisk together the flours, remaining 24 g (2 tablespoons) sugar, baking powder, and salt. Stir in the milk and yogurt to form a dough. Drop 2 heaping tablespoons (100 g) of dough on the top of each bowl of fruit, slightly spreading it so the top will bake evenly.

Bake for 20 to 24 minutes, until golden. If using the 9-inch (23 cm) baking pan, bake for 30 to 35 minutes. Serve warm or at room temperature.

Yield: 4 cobblers

Recipe Note

Because different types of fruit have different levels of sweetness, be sure to taste the fruit mixture before removing it from the heat, and add extra sugar to taste. They also have different juice levels, so add more cornstarch if needed.

Chocolate Raspberry Tart

Rich and creamy, this decadent tart could be served in a five-star vegan restaurant. With only ½ teaspoon oil per serving, this raspberry chocolate explosion lets you pamper yourself and your family without the guilt.

• •

FOR CRUST:

Nonstick cooking spray

40 g (½ cup) quick-cooking oats

60 g (½ cup) whole wheat pastry flour

10 g (2 tablespoons) unsweetened cocoa powder

1 teaspoon instant espresso granules

2 tablespoons (30 ml) pure maple syrup

1 tablespoon (15 ml) neutral-flavored oil

1 tablespoon (15 ml) water, more if needed

FOR FILLING AND TOPPING:

105 g (¾ cup) cashews, soaked in cold water for 3 hours, drained, and patted dry

¼ cup plus 2 tablespoons (90 ml) vegan creamer, preferably Silk or MimicCreme brand

20 g (¼ cup) unsweetened cocoa powder

60 g (3 tablespoons) all-fruit raspberry jam

2 tablespoons (30 ml) pure maple syrup

190 g (1½ cups) fresh raspberries

TO MAKE THE CRUST: Preheat the oven to 350°F (180°C, or gas mark 4). Lightly coat a 6½-inch (16 cm) tart pan with cooking spray.

Combine the oats, flour, cocoa, and espresso granules in a small bowl. Stir in the syrup, oil, and water. The mixture will be sticky and should hold its shape when pressed together. If not, add more water, 1 teaspoon at a time, until it does. Press the mixture evenly onto the sides and bottom of the tart pan. Dampening your hands with water may help reduce some of the sticking. Put the tart pan on a baking sheet. Bake the crust for 7 to 8 minutes, until the edges start to look dry. Let cool on a wire rack for 1 hour, or until completely cool.

TO MAKE THE FILLING: Combine the cashews, creamer, cocoa, jam, and maple syrup in a blender. Process until completely smooth. Spread the filling evenly in the prepared tart shell. Top with the raspberries, beginning at the outer edge of the tart and working in circles toward the center.

Chill for 3 hours before serving.

Yield: One 6½-inch (16 cm) tart

Recipe Note

This recipe can also be made in three 4-inch (10 cm) tart pans. You may have a small amount of filling left over; it can be chilled and eaten as mousse.

Whole Wheat Lemon Tartlets

Most of our testers found these delicious tartlets to be at their best using only the amount of lemon juice noted in the recipe, but a couple of other folks (including ourselves) prefer to use 1 cup (235 ml) lemon juice and no water, for tarter results. We suggest trying the recipe as it is written first, and tweaking the amount of juice and water to your liking the next time you make it. If you're looking for an extra kick to pair up with that lemon flavor, be sure to see the curd variations on pages 46 and 148.

● ●

FOR CRUST:

Nonstick cooking spray

90 g (¾ cup) whole wheat pastry flour

35 g (¼ cup) raw cashews

Pinch of fine sea salt

2 tablespoons (30 ml) pure maple syrup or (42 g) raw agave nectar

2 to 3 tablespoons (30 to 45 ml) melted coconut oil

FOR LEMON CURD:

⅔ cup (160 ml) fresh lemon juice

⅓ cup plus 2 tablespoons (110 ml) water, divided

70 g (½ cup) raw cashews, soaked in cold water for 3 hours, drained, and patted dry

⅔ cup (160 ml) pure maple syrup or (222 g) raw agave nectar

16 g (2 tablespoons) cornstarch

Fresh raspberries, for garnish (optional)

TO MAKE THE CRUST: Preheat the oven to 325°F (170°C, or gas mark 3). Lightly coat six 3-inch (8 cm) fluted French tart pans with cooking spray.

Combine the flour, cashews, and salt in a food processor. Process until the cashews are finely ground. Add the maple syrup and 2 tablespoons (30 ml) of the oil at first, pulsing to combine. Add the remaining 1 tablespoon (15 ml) oil if the dough crumbs do not hold together when pinched.

Knead a few times and divide the dough into 6 equal portions. Press down each portion into each prepared pan to evenly cover the bottom and sides. Use the tines of a fork to lightly prick each crust bottom.

Bake for 10 to 12 minutes, until light golden brown. Place on a wire rack to cool. Once the pans are cool enough to handle, carefully pop the crusts out of the pans, and let the crusts cool completely on the rack.

TO MAKE THE LEMON CURD: Combine the lemon juice, ⅓ cup (80 ml) of the water, cashews, and maple syrup in a blender. Blend until perfectly smooth. Pass through a fine-mesh sieve, if needed, to remove any pieces of cashew still remaining. Transfer to a small saucepan, and bring to a boil over high heat.

Combine the cornstarch and the remaining 2 tablespoons (30 ml) water in a small bowl to create a slurry. Lower the heat of the lemon mixture, add the cornstarch slurry while stirring constantly, and cook over medium heat until slightly thickened, about 2 minutes. Remove from the heat, still stirring, and let cool.

Stir the curd again once it's cooled. Spoon the curd into the tarts. Garnish with fresh berries, if desired. These are best served chilled from the refrigerator, and enjoyed within a day of preparation. Store any leftover curd in a jar in the refrigerator.

Yield: 6 tartlets, heaping 1½ cups (540 g) curd

About the Authors

Celine Steen is the coauthor of *500 Vegan Recipes*, *The Complete Guide to Vegan Food Substitutions*, *Hearty Vegan Meals for Monster Appetites*, and *Vegan Sandwiches Save the Day!* You can find her at www.havecakewilltravel.com and contact her at celine@havecakewilltravel.com.

Tami Noyes is the author of *American Vegan Kitchen* and *Grills Gone Vegan* and the coauthor of *Vegan Sandwiches Save the Day!* She lives, cooks, and blogs in her two-kitty home in Ohio. In addition to her blog, www.veganappetite.com, Tami contributes to several vegan sites. Email Tami at veganappetite@gmail.com.

Acknowledgments

Our eternal gratitude goes to Amanda Waddell, Meg Baskis, Betsy Gammons, Karen Levy, Liz Jones, and Megan Jones for their impeccable professionalism and boundless awesomeness!

The Best Testers Ever awards go to: Courtney Blair, Monika Soria Caruso, Kelly and Mac Cavalier (who tested about a million recipes), Michelle Cavigliano, Shannon Davis, Anna Holt and sons, Shelly Mocquet-McDonald, Monique and Michel Narbel-Gimzia, Constanze Reichardt, and Vegan Aide. Thank you for sharing your time, your kitchens, and your ideas to help make this a better book.

Tami would like to thank Jim (it all started with cookies!), her family, the love cats, and of course, Celine, for this incredible bake-venture!

Celine is as always beyond grateful for the love and support of Chaz and her parents. High-fives to Tami for another fun-tastic cookbook-writing session.

Index